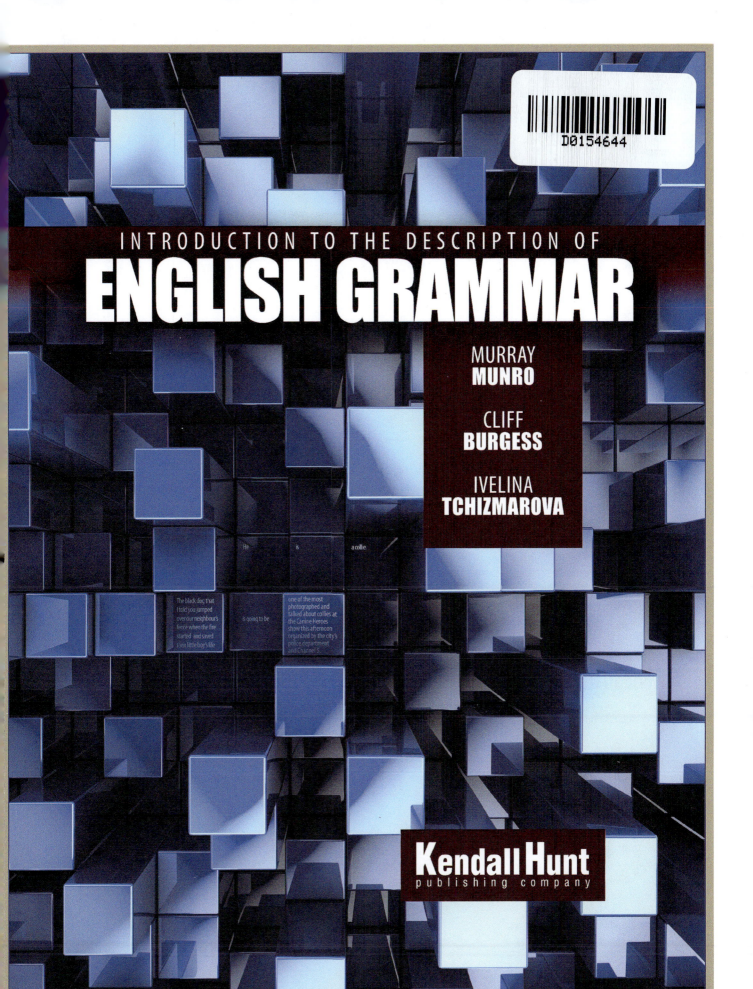

INTRODUCTION TO THE DESCRIPTION OF

ENGLISH GRAMMAR

MURRAY
MUNRO

CLIFF
BURGESS

IVELINA
TCHIZMAROVA

Kendall Hunt
publishing company

Kendall Hunt
publishing company

www.kendallhunt.com
Send all inquiries to:
4050 Westmark Drive
Dubuque, IA 52004-1840

Copyright © 2011 by Kendall Hunt Publishing Company

ISBN 978-1-4652-0542-1

Printed in the United States of America
10 9 8 7 6 5 4 3 2

We would like to express our deepest gratitude to Margaret Bru, Ryan Schrodt, and everyone else at Kendall Hunt Publishing for their professionalism, advice, and enthusiastic support for our work on this textbook.

We would also like to thank the Department of Linguistics at Simon Fraser University which brought us together.

We dedicate this book to our families, who have embraced our passion for language.

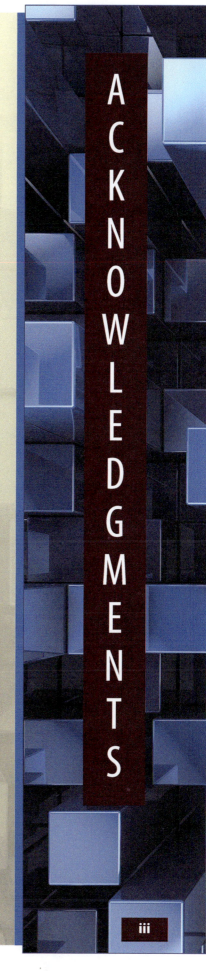

ACKNOWLEDGMENTS

CONTENTS

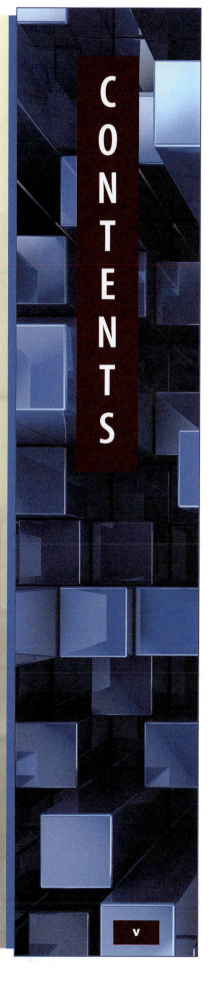

v

What is Grammar?

For linguists, the study of *grammar* is the study of the structure of language. In its broadest sense, *grammar* covers a wide variety of phenomena including the sound system of a language; the lexicon, which consists of words and other meaningful units; and larger structures such as phrases and sentences. However, *grammar* also has a more restricted sense—the one that we will use in this book. When most of us think of grammar, we think of the structure of sentences. When we "do" grammar, we analyze this structure by parsing (identifying the categories to which words belong) and by describing how the words form recurring patterns that we call *phrases* and *clauses.* There are many different approaches to grammar. The sections that follow outline some of them.

Descriptive Grammar

The material covered in this book is presented from a descriptive perspective. We will *describe* English sentence structure by examining the ways in which proficient speakers of English use grammar. When we take this view of language, we do *not* think of utterances in terms of whether they are *good* or *bad* English. Instead, we are concerned with the ways in which sentences and other units are commonly constructed. *Grammatical* sentences are structures that proficient speakers of English would actually say or write. In English, for example, determiners like *the* come before the nouns that they refer to. So we might say that a descriptive "fact" or "rule" of English grammar is that determiners precede nouns. If you compare sentences 1 and 2 below, you'll notice that the first one conforms to that expectation, while the second one does not. For that reason we consider the first sentence to be grammatical and the second one to be ungrammatical. To denote an ungrammatical structure, linguists typically use an asterisk as shown.

1) The cat was sleeping by the door.
2) *Cat the was sleeping by door the.

Sentence 2 above is ungrammatical because its word order doesn't fit our expectations about the way English sentences are constructed. However, word order is not the only thing we need to consider when analyzing grammatical structure. Sentence 3 below is grammatical, while 4 is not:

3) She works at the bakery.
4) *She work at the bakery.

The problem with sentence 4 is that it lacks a marker (*-s*) that is required in present-tense sentences with *he* or *she* as a subject. Still another example of ungrammaticality is illustrated by the following pair:

5) I ate all my dinner.
6) *I eated all my dinner.

This time, the problem has to do with a particular verb form. The past form of *eat* is *ate,* not *eated.* Children sometimes produce sentences like 6 when they are acquiring English, probably because they have recognized that many past tense verbs have an *-ed* ending. However, they eventually learn to produce the grammatical form *ate.*

While proficient speakers of English generally agree that sentences 2, 4, and 6 are ungrammatical, sometimes there are differences of opinion about other structures. One thing to notice is that the grammaticality of an utterance depends on the particular variety or dialect of a language that is being considered. In other words, a sentence that is grammatical in one variety of English may not be grammatical in another. For most speakers of Western Canadian English (WCE) the following are not grammatical:

7) *I might could get some eggs when I go to the store.
8) *This chair needs fixed.

Sentence 7 is marked with an asterisk because WCE generally does not allow more than one modal auxiliary (a word like *can, may, might,* or *could*) in a verb unit. Sentence 8 is also ungrammatical because, in WCE, *needs* requires an *-ing* form as its complement. Most speakers of WCE find both these sentences unacceptable and would be unlikely to ever say or write them. However, in some varieties of English, including dialects spoken in the southern United States, both of these sentences are grammatical, and a linguist attempting to describe those varieties would *not* mark them with an asterisk. In this book we will use WCE as our basis for deciding what is and what is not grammatical. We will focus on sentences that are clearly grammatical and will occasionally consider ones that are clearly ungrammatical. Sometimes speakers of a particular variety of a language like WCE may disagree on whether or not a particular sentence is grammatical. We will leave these debatable cases for discussion elsewhere.

One can approach descriptive grammar in a variety of ways. Linguists have developed many different types of labels and diagrams for sentences. Their variable approaches to grammar often make different assumptions about the nature of linguistic structures. In this book, we will take a traditional approach—one that uses fairly well-known labels in commonly-accepted ways. In fact, much of the terminology we will cover is similar to that used in books written for learners of English as a second language. However, if you read other books about language structure, you will find that the terminology used to talk about grammar can vary, and that different principles of analysis are often assumed. Some approaches require a strict formalism: labels are applied in very particular ways, and tree diagrams are used to illustrate subtle structural phenomena. While the purpose of this book is to help you approach English grammar analytically, our goal is not to learn a particular formalism or to draw tree diagrams simply for the sake of doing so. Rather, we will aim at a general overview of English structures that should help you understand virtually any basic English grammar text.

The existence of a wide variety of approaches to English grammar reflects the fact that linguists have not come to an agreement on the best way to characterize the structure of English—or of languages in general. If you are to be successful at language analysis, you will have to accept this fact.

Prescriptive Grammar

Prescriptive grammar entails the evaluation of particular ways of using language as *correct* or *incorrect* or as *good* or *bad*. People who take this view use their opinions about language to tell others how to speak or write. Someone who tells you not to end a sentence with a preposition or not to "split" an infinitive (as in "to quickly finish") is prescribing, rather than describing language use. This is a very different way of thinking about language than the *descriptive* approach covered above. Descriptivists consider all structures that proficient speakers systematically use to be grammatical. (Of course, that doesn't include sentences produced with speech errors.) Therefore, for descriptivists, *ungrammatical* structures are ones that people *don't* use. Prescriptivists, on the other hand, take the view that even things that people regularly say or write should be judged as *good* or *bad*. Over the centuries, hundreds of prescriptive "rules" have been proposed for English. Here are a few:

- *Don't end an utterance with a preposition.* Some people claim that "Who were you talking to?" is inferior to "To whom were you talking?"
- *Don't split an infinitive.* They might also claim that ". . . to boldly go where no man has gone before . . ." is inferior to " . . . to go boldly where no man has gone before . . ."
- *Don't use object forms after BE.* They might insist that "It's me" should be replaced by "It is I."
- *Don't use "if" to begin a noun complement clause.* They might say that "I wonder if he's coming" is not as good as "I wonder whether he is coming."

Even though some prescriptivists object to the examples above, we have not used any asterisks, because these patterns are not ungrammatical. In fact, proficient English speakers use structures like these all the time. Because the field of linguistics aims at documenting and analyzing the way language is actually used, rather than at telling people how to speak or write, linguists generally take a negative view of prescriptivism. In fact, some linguists have written quite scathing criticisms of prescriptivist thinking. In this text, we will certainly not be taking a prescriptive approach. However, it is worth commenting briefly on some of the errors in thinking that underlie a great deal of prescriptivist commentary on language.

Emotional Responses to Language

Some people believe that their own negative emotional reactions to particular uses of language should be shared by everyone. For instance, you might hear them complaining that they are horrified when they hear "access" used as a verb, as in "Everyone can access that web page easily." Other folks become emotional about sentence-final prepositions or split infinitives. Regrettably, the people who become most emotional about language are often those who have the least understanding of linguistics. One very famous example of linguistic emotionalism comes from George Orwell, author of the novels *Animal Farm* and *1984.* In 1946, Orwell wrote a bombastic essay entitled *Politics and the English Language,* in which he presented some of his prejudices about language use. Among these was his prescriptive belief that the passive voice should be avoided as much as possible. Orwell, who was not the first person to complain about the passive, would probably claim, for instance, that a sentence like "The house was damaged by the storm." is inferior to "The storm damaged the house." A number of years later an analysis of Orwell's essay was published, in which it was reported that more than 20% of the verbs in that very essay were in the passive voice. Yet in typical periodical writing, the frequency of passive use was only about 13%! As far as anyone knows, Orwell was unaware that he was violating his own rule over and over again, and that he was actually using the passive *more* often than other writers. A possible reason for the discrepancy between his advice and his actions is that Orwell had not reflected carefully on the uses of the English passive. Instead his ideas were motivated by emotionalism. Descriptive linguists do not regard the passive as "good" or "bad." Instead, they point out that the passive voice is generally used when the doer of an action is unknown or relatively unimportant. In scientific writing, for instance, the passive allows a writer to economically refer to actions and events without mentioning the agent (for instance, "The patient was given an injection" instead of "A nurse gave an injection to the patient.") This case, and many others like it, have been discussed at length by the linguist, Geoffrey Pullum. You can read more of his ideas at the *Language Log* website <http://languagelog.ldc.upenn.edu/nll/>.

Misinformed and Illogical Views about Language

Some popular ideas about language are based on misinformation or a lack of understanding of how languages work. Some prescriptivists believe, for example, that older language forms and meanings are inherently more "correct" than newer ones. For instance, some have claimed that the expression "comprised of" is less correct than "comprised" because the first form appeared later in the development of English (around the end of the eighteenth century CE). They argue that instead of saying "Canada is comprised of ten provinces" you should say "Canada comprises ten provinces." However, if we were to follow this type of reasoning to its logical end, we would have to conclude that almost all aspects of contemporary English are wrong! English has changed a great deal over the many centuries that it has existed as a language. Here, for instance, is a passage written in Old English, a phase of the language that lasted from about the fifth century to twelfth century CE:

> Eft he axode, hu ðære ðeode nama wære þe hi of comon. Him wæs geandwyrd, þæt hi Angle genemnode wæron. Þa cwæð he, "Rihtlice hi sind Angle gehatene, for ðan ðe hi engla wlite habbað, and swilcum gedafenað Þæt hi on heofonum engla geferan beon." (Source: Merriam-Webster Online Dictionary <http://www.merriam-webster.com/help/faq/history.htm>)

As you can see, this passage is mostly unintelligible to users of modern-day English. But if it really were true that older forms of language are "more correct" than newer forms, we would have to say that this passage is better written than its contemporary translation. Perhaps that means that we should all go back to speaking Old English to ensure that we are using our language correctly! Of course, that is a ridiculous idea, but it appears to be a logical extension of the belief that "older is better."

The idea that older forms are inherently better than new ones is based on the false assumption that languages cannot evolve over time. In fact, all languages change, and it is unlikely that prescriptivists (or anyone else) can do anything to prevent this from happening. Descriptivists accept this fact. Moreover, they do not see linguistic change as inherently good or bad.

Another example of misinformed reasoning about language concerns the use of *their* as a singular possessive word, as in the following sentence:

9)   Everyone should do their best.

Notice that we have not used an asterisk because this is a common type of utterance in WCE and in other varieties of English. However, prescriptivists have sometimes argued that sentence 9 is "bad English." They note that *everyone* is a singular pronoun, but claim that *their* is a plural determiner that cannot be used to refer to a singular antecedent. This notion about correct and incorrect uses of *their* was probably the idea of eighteenth century grammarians, and it has been a favourite issue of grade school English teachers for a very long time. Some people have even argued that the occurrence of sentences like sentence 9 shows that English grammar is deteriorating and that the language is "at risk." However, there is no reason to take that view seriously. Prior to the eighteenth century CE, *their* was commonly used with a singular antecedent, and you will find examples of this usage in the writings of Shakespeare, Chaucer, Swift, and many other great writers. If English really were in decline, it would seem odd to put the blame on Shakespeare!

Rather than view the plural use of *their* as a sign of bad English, descriptivists prefer to look for reasons why speakers of English might make such a choice. A likely explanation is that the alternatives to using *their* in sentence 9 are not very satisfactory. English has a few third person possessives: *his, her, its,* and *one's,* for example. What problems do you see with each of these possibilities?

Stylebooks and writing manuals usually treat language prescriptively. Their authors might argue that written English is clearer and easier to read when certain prescriptions are followed. Whether they are right on that point is an issue that could be discussed at great length. However, we will not focus our attention on prescriptive matters in this book.

Punctuation is not Grammar!

Issues of punctuation and spelling are not regarded as aspects of descriptive grammar, and we will not generally discuss them either. A sentence like "*Studying grammer sure is interesting*" is not ungrammatical, even though it does contain a spelling error and lacks punctuation.

Applied Grammar: Teaching Second Language Learners

Applied grammar is the approach to grammar used in second language instruction. If you have learned English, French, or Mandarin as a second language, you have probably used a "pedagogical grammar" textbook. Most second language teaching is based on descriptive, rather than prescriptive, accounts of language. Although language teachers certainly give their students advice on how sentences are formed, their goal is to help learners gain proficiency in the language being taught. Therefore, they usually encourage their students to speak and write the language the way proficient users do. For instance, ESL instructors might teach students that sentence 10 below is grammatical, whereas 11 is not:

10)   He often takes the bus to work.
11)   *He takes often the bus to work.

Proficient speakers of English will almost always agree that something is wrong with sentence 11, although they might not be able to explain why. In this case, the problem has to do with the position of the frequency adverb *often*. Frequency adverbs do not generally occur between a verb *(takes)* and a direct object *(the bus)*.

Most ESL instructors base their teaching on descriptive English grammar and not on prescriptions about good and bad usage. In a discussion between two ESL teachers a number of years ago, one of them mentioned that he had been telling his students about the common use of *There's...* in both singular and plural contexts. For instance, some proficient speakers of English might use all the following:

12)   There's a fly in my soup.
13)   There are three people in the room.
14)   There's three people in the room.
15)   There's a lot of cars parked on the street.

The other teacher was surprised that sentences 14 and 15 had been recommended to the students because she thought that these illustrated "bad" English. "Do you teach your students what English speakers *actually* say or what they *should* say?" she asked. As you can readily see, she was taking a prescriptive view. The reply was that the most important thing in English language instruction is to teach actual usage. Moreover, it would be useful to point out to students the difference in the ways sentences 13 and 14 might be used. If you were faced with the same situation, how would you explain the difference between these two utterances?

Grammar and Psychology

Some linguists study the ways in which linguistic knowledge is represented in the minds of speakers. They aim at answering the question "What do you know when you know a language?" Addressing this problem has led to much debate. For instance, some scholars have argued that a great deal of human knowledge of language is innately endowed. According to that account, we are born programmed with a universal grammar that includes quite specific information about how languages work. If so, then the chief task of children learning a native language is to discover how universal grammar is applied in that language.

But the *nativist* view of language described above is just one perspective. Other contemporary researchers and theorists doubt the existence of this kind of universal grammar. Instead, they believe that all the important aspects of language have to be learned after birth. They place the focus on how children make use of the linguistic input that they hear from caregivers and others in order to become proficient users of language.

Some linguists carry out psycholinguistic research to address this controversy and to answer other questions about the psychology of language. They might, for example, observe that sentences like 16 are sometimes produced by children learning English as a first language or by ESL learners:

16)   *She goed home already.

This sentence uses a past tense form (*goed), which looks very much like many common past tense forms (*arrived, lived, fixed,* etc.), but which adult English speakers recognize as ungrammatical. The *overgeneralization* of the -ed past tense marker to an inappropriate situation is a common process in language acquisition. Psycholinguists are interested in explaining why such errors occur. One possible account is that people acquire and use subconscious structural "rules" about language, which they sometimes misapply. On that view, one of the things language learners must do is to learn when and when not to apply particular rules. In the case of the past tense, for instance, one might say that learners acquire a rule that captures the way the *–ed* marker is used, and that they must apply that rule only to certain verbs like *wait* and *need,* but not to the verbs *eat, drive,* and *write.*

However, an account based on rules is only one possible way of understanding why language learners make this error. Other linguists have proposed different kinds of language acquisition processes that do not entail actual knowledge of rules, but which have to do with the way the people *associate* different kinds of information in their brains. They argue that extensive exposure to and experience with a language results in a complex array of neural connections in the brain. It is these connections that underlie our ability to produce language that is grammatical. While a great deal of attention is currently being devoted to this newer viewpoint on language, it is likely that the debate over this problem and other related issues will continue for many years into the future.

Things You Need to Know About
Descriptive vs. Prescriptive Grammar

Descriptive Rules (D-rules)	Prescriptive Rules (P-rules)	1

Descriptive Rules (D-rules)

- Describe language as it is spoken by proficient adult native speakers of English; e.g.,

  - In English, personal pronouns appear as object forms after prepositions (between you and me, about me, *between you and I, *about I).
  - In English the adjective is normally placed before the noun (beautiful place, *place beautiful).
  - In English statements (but not in questions) the subject normally precedes the verb (she laughed, *laughed she).

- Describe objectively sentences (1)–(4) as they occur in English (e.g., (1) and (3) as less formal than (2) and (4)), without qualifying any of them as "more correct" than the others.

  (1) Who is she going out with?
  (2) With whom is she going out?
  (3) This is the man (that/who) I told you about.
  (4) This is the man about whom I told you.

Prescriptive Rules (P-rules)

- Do **not** describe how language is actually used but rather prescribe how it should be used in someone's opinion; e.g., one P-rule states that:

  - We should say "between you and I" despite the fact that most native speakers (correctly) say "between you and me."

- Reflect people's preferences about the best way to say something when several alternative expressions are available.

  (1) $\boxed{*P}$ Who is she going out with? violates the P-rules:
  (a) "Do not end sentences with prepositions," and
  (b) "Use 'whom,' not 'who' in object position".

  (2) With whom is she going out? conforms to P-rules.

- Entail subjective evaluation or judgment, someone's preference about "good" and "bad," "correct" or "incorrect" language; according to these rules:

  (3) $\boxed{*P}$ This is the man (that/who) I told you about.
  is "bad/incorrect . . . " English; while,
  (4) This is the man about whom I told you.
  is "good/proper . . . " English.

Things You Need to Know About
Descriptive vs. Prescriptive Grammar

Descriptive Rules (D-rules)	Prescriptive Rules (P-rules)	2

- Are learned naturally by native speakers, usually at home. Native speakers would say (5), but not (6):

  (5) My computer broke down last night.
  (6) *Computer my broke down last night.

  - Sentence (6) violates a D-rule: "The possessive pro-determiner should be placed before the noun in English."
  - Native speakers do **not** produce sentences like (6); therefore this rule describes actual usage (and does **not** need to be taught at school).

- Comply with historical facts (based on Crystal 1995:44, 79, 367):

  - The use of sentences ending in prepositions, beginning with conjunctions, or containing split infinitives (e.g., to quickly finish something) is evident in the works of the most educated people and renowned English writers such as Milton, Shakespeare and Locke.
  - Using multiple negation for emphasis has been a natural part of the English language since Old English.

- Reflect the understanding that beginning sentences with conjunctions such as '*and*' may not be acceptable in some styles and registers; e.g., formal written academic prose, but in informal spoken English many utterances start this way, and, indeed, this is the most natural way to speak English.

- Allow all four sentences below:

  (8) There'**s** a bear on the road.
  (9) There **are two bears** on the road.
  (10) **There's** two bears on the road.
  (11) There's a lot of bears in the forest.

- Are **not** learned naturally by native speakers but have to be learned later in life; e.g., at school.

- Contradict not only actual modern usage but also historical facts about the English language.

- Often mix up levels of formality and style with grammaticality and accuracy; e.g.,

  (7) *P And then she came to me, and gave me the letter. And I asked her …
  violates the P-rule:
  "Do not start sentences with conjunctions."

- Fail to account for language change as in sentences (10) and (12), and/or apply rules consistently as in (11):

  (8) There'**s** a bear on the road.
  (9) There **are** two bears on the road.
  (10) *P There'**s two bears** on the road.
  (11) There's a lot of bears in the forest.

Things You Need to Know About
Descriptive vs. Prescriptive Grammar

Descriptive Rules (D-rules)	Prescriptive Rules (P-rules) 3
Sentence (10) contains an innovative form where the verb ("be"-singular) agrees with the impersonal existential "there" subject, rather than with the predicate noun (also called *predicate nominative*) (plural "two bears"; cf. (9)).	Sentence (10) violates P-rule: Verbs must always agree in number with the predicate nouns/subject complements.

Descriptive Rules continued:

(12) **Everyone** should do **their** best.
Allow this structure along with other alternatives, and reanalyzes "their" as a neutral possessive determiner used:

- when it's not necessary or possible to determine gender, and
- instead of the longer and more cumbersome "his or her" (especially when it has to be repeated several times in a paragraph).

- Articles and books on language written by linguists, and many newer grammar and ESL texts are concerned only with D-rules. If P-rules are mentioned at all, it is only to show why they do **not** reflect language use and language change accurately.

Prescriptive Rules continued:

- Do not sanction (11) as a P-rule violation although the verb ("be") agrees with the prearticle ("**a** lot of") rather than with the head noun ("bears") in the NP.

(12) [*P] **Everyone** should do **their** best. violates the P-rule:
Possessive pronoun determiners must agree in number with their antecedents. The P-rule requires that "their" be made singular ("one's", or "his or her"), or "everyone" be changed to plural ("people").

- Writing manuals, some traditional grammar and ESL texts, and the spell checker of your computer contain numerous P-rules.

Exercises

A. Indicate whether each of the statements below is motivated by descriptive (D) or prescriptive (P) thinking.

    _____ **1.** In English, adverbs often end in *-ly*.

    _____ **2.** It really burns me up when people say *irregardless* when they mean *regardless*.

    _____ **3.** The sentence "Don't gives that to me" is not well-formed in WCE.

    _____ **4.** People who say *"Wazzup?"* don't know proper English.

    _____ **5.** Children need to study grammar in school so that they learn to speak correctly.

B. Place an '*' in front of each sentence that is **ungrammatical** for most or all proficient speakers of Western Canadian English (WCE), and see if you can explain why (i.e. explains how they violate D-rules). Then indicate which sentences might be criticized by a prescriptivist, despite being grammatical?

1. Be sure to fully cook the turkey.

    _____

    _____

    _____

2. Colourless green ideas sleep furiously.

    _____

    _____

    _____

3. Why do he always leave the lights on?

    _____

    _____

    _____

4. The people which live in that house are extremely tidy.

_____

_____

_____

5. Because of the turbulence, you'll have to fasten your seatbelt.

_____

_____

_____

6. She drinks always coffee for breakfast.

_____

_____

_____

7. did you here the good, news.

_____

_____

_____

8. Some people dislike to go out in the rain.

_____

_____

_____

C. All of the following are grammatical in some variety of English, but are unlikely to be used by speakers of WCE. Why not?

1. These drawings are not identical; one is clearly different to the other.

_____

_____

2. What are y'all doing after the movie?

_____

_____

3. She graduated high school in 2006.

_____

_____

4. He all right!

_____

_____

5. He was standing on line at the theatre for over an hour.

_____

_____

6. Beloved, thou hast brought me many flowers plucked in the garden.

_____

_____

D. The following utterances have been made by native speakers of English. If you think that some of them may be criticized by prescriptivists, write down "**Yes**" (= 'likely to be criticized') next to the sentence number in the first column of the table, and then provide a brief explanation in the second column, as in the example below. If you think that a sentence does not violate prescriptive grammar rules, write down "**No**" (= 'not likely to be criticized') next to that sentence number as in sentence (2) in the example below.

Example:

1. Say you don't need no money and I'll be satisfied.

2. The electronic paper has a different layout from the printed version.

Answer:

Sentence #	Explanation
1. Yes	Double negative
2. No	_____

1. I don't know who they got the information from, but it's not true.

2. The goal of most international students is to quickly learn the language of instruction in the host country.

3. Contrary to parents' beliefs, every teenager knows what is best for them.

4. My boss always answers with "We'll see."

5. There's no secrets between me and you.

6. This is the bestest thing that could have happened to you.

7. Dr. Atkins never accepts late papers.

8. There's never been so many graduate students in the department.

9. If someone calls this afternoon, don't forget to ask for their phone number.

10. I think they are talking about you and I.

11. Hi guys, I'll be keen to attend the meeting. See youse all then.

12. And he's like, "Could you, like, give me, like, $5.00?"

Example #	Explanation
	According to prescriptive rules only. (Note that according to the descriptive view, these sentences are acceptable.)
1.	
2.	
3.	
4.	
5.	
6.	
7.	
8.	
9.	
10.	
11.	
12.	

Answers to Exercises

Exercise A:

1. D   **2.** P   **3.** D   **4.** P   **5.** P

Exercise B:

Descriptive rules:

3. * "do" should be "do**es**" (third person singular ending)
4. * "the people **which**" (inanimate) should be "the people **who**" (animate)
6. * drinks **always** coffee" [Verb + Adverb (Frequency) + Direct Object] should be "**always** drinks coffee" [Adverb (Frequency) + Verb + Direct Object] (adverbs of frequency do not occur between the verb and its direct object)
8. * "dislike **to go**" should be "dislike **going**" ("dislike" takes gerunds, not infinitives)

Note: Sentence 2 is meaningless but fully grammatical (hence, no *).
Sentence 7 has spelling, punctuation, and capitalization errors, but no D-errors.

Exercise C:

Origin of Utterances

1. British English
2. Southern US English
3. US English
4. AAVE (African-American Vernacular English) and hip-hop
5. some US dialects
6. Elizabeth Barrett Browning, a prominent Victorian poet (1806-1861).

Exercise D:

Example #	Explanation
	According to prescriptive rules only. (Note that according to the descriptive view, these sentences are acceptable.)
1. Yes	The prep *from* should be moved before the word *who*, **and** *who* should be changed to *whom* in object position *(. . . from whom they got the information . . .)*.
2. Yes	The adverb *quickly* should not split the infinitive.
3. Yes	*Every* is singular, so *them* should be singular *(him or her)* to agree with its antecedent.
4. No	_____

5. Yes	The verb *'s* should be changed to *are* to agree with plural *secrets.*	
6. Yes	Wrong superlative degree of adjective: "the bestest" has double marking [should be "the best"].	
7. No	_____	
8. Yes	The verb *'s* should be changed to *have* to agree with plural *so many graduate students.*	
9. Yes	*Someone* is singular, so *their* should be singular *(his or her)* to agree with its antecedent.	
10. No	This one is interesting! Although many prescriptivists will not criticise it, it is actually **ungrammatical according to descriptive rules.** The personal pronouns should be in their object forms after the preposition *about;* i.e, *about you and me.* This is a case of the so-called "hypercorrection."	
11. Yes	The non-standard/dialectal form "youse" should be changed to "you."	
12. Yes	Overuse of the word "like" in non-standard ways. "He's like" should be changed to "he said," and the other two instances of "like" should be deleted.	

Classifying Words

CHAPTER

2

Word classes fall into two broad categories: open classes (nouns, verbs, adjectives, and adverbs) and closed classes (everything else). The sections that follow present some of the labels that we will be using for words when we analyze the structure of English sentences. For instance, we'll use **'N'** for a noun and **'Adj'** for an adjective. Doing this type of analysis is called *parsing,* and we'll refer to the labels in this section as *parsing labels.* In most cases we will be using the same symbols that Morenberg (2010) uses. However, we will add a few items to his list.

Open Classes

A class is regarded as "open" when new words can be added to it quite readily. For instance, as English changes in response to developments in technology, medicine, politics, and culture, we get new words like *iPod, Viagra, ringtone, unibrow, supersize,* or *pwned.* Words from open classes carry most of the meaningful content of a sentence. In fact, well-formed English sentences usually contain at least one open class word. For that reason, they are sometimes called *content words.*

Nouns (N)

Reference

Nouns are commonly said to refer to:

people	Marie-France, doctor, professor
places	Victoria, Stanley Park
things	tree, cat, soup

However, that definition is not very satisfactory. *Nothingness* is a noun, but it doesn't fit into any of those categories. And abstract concepts like *honesty, evil,* and *beauty* are certainly not "things" in the same sense that a *tree* is a thing. For these reasons, it is helpful to think of word classes not just in terms of their reference, but also in terms of the roles they can play in sentences. Here we can use "slot tests" that may help us identify the class of a word on the basis of its grammatical properties. Because a noun, or a noun with a determiner, can serve as the subject or object of a sentence, words that fit grammatically into the blanks below are likely to be nouns:

Slot Tests

(The) _____ is interesting.
I like (the) _____ .
I hate (the) _____ .

Nouns can be sub-categorized according to three types of distinctions, as outlined below.

Noun Sub-Classes

a) Countable vs. uncountable nouns

<u>Countable nouns</u> refer to entities that can be enumerated (one cat, two cats, three cats, etc.); therefore, countable nouns have both singular and plural forms. Most nouns can be used in a countable sense in at least some circumstances.

card(s)   box(es)   chair(s)

<u>Uncountable or mass nouns</u> refer to things that are not generally regarded as individual entities. Nouns used in a mass sense are not pluralized.

milk   air   hydrogen

b) Proper vs. common nouns

<u>Proper nouns (PropN)</u> refer to specific people, places, or things and are usually capitalized.

Paris   Mr. Bean   the Vatican

<u>Common nouns</u> refer to everyday things.

magazine   bean   telephone

c) Concrete vs. abstract nouns

<u>Concrete nouns</u> refer to things that can be seen, touched, or otherwise experienced directly through the senses.

rock   fence   water

Abstract nouns refer to qualities or ideas that cannot be experienced directly by seeing, touching, etc. These nouns are not commonly pluralized.

> love   stupidity   hatred

Note that the three sub-classes are not mutually exclusive. For instance, a concrete noun may simultaneously be a countable noun.

Verbs

Later on, we will be using a variety of different parsing labels for verbs. For now, we will simply call them **'V.'**

Reference

Verbs are sometimes described as "action words":

actions	Tracey **works** seven days a week.
	Harry **got up** at six.
	Fido **chased** the car around the block.

However, many verbs do not refer to actions at all. Some verbs describe the following:

states/characteristics	Ludo **seems** tired.
	The president **became** a tyrant.
sensations	This durian **smells** terrible.

Still other verbs don't fit any of these categories very well:

> Lyman **has** a lot of time to kill.
> Lionel **endured** the two-hour operation.

As with nouns, it is often helpful to verify that a word is a verb by examining its grammatical properties. Because the auxiliary *can* is used together with verbs, words that fit into the following slots are likely to be verbs.

Slot Tests

> I can _____ (it) (there).
> It can _____ .
> It can _____ good.

Sub-Classes

There are many sub-classes of verbs. We will discuss these extensively later on.

Adjectives (Adj)

Reference
Adjectives are sometimes said to "modify" or supply descriptive information about nouns. They may answer such questions as "what kind" or indicate a characteristic or state of something.

> This morning, I saw a **pretty** bird.
> The weather last spring was **awful**.

Slot Tests
Grammatically speaking, adjectives pattern in two distinct ways. An *attributive adjective* is one that immediately precedes the noun that it refers to.

> *Attributive Adjective:* A **huge** tree is growing on our front lawn.

A predicate adjective generally follows the verb in a sentence, and the noun it refers to comes earlier.

> *Predicate Adjective:* Linda was **enthusiastic**.

Words that can fill one or both of the slots below are likely to be adjectives:

> (The) _____ [noun] was very interesting.   (attributive slot)
> (The) [noun] was very _____ .   (predicate slot)

Adverbs (Adv)

Reference
People often say that adverbs modify verbs, but that is not a very satisfactory description of their use. Often, adverbs provide background information for an entire sentence and are not tied to any other single word. They generally answer such questions as "how," "how often," "when," and "where." They are associated with the following types of meanings (among others).

manner	quickly, slowly
time	yesterday, tomorrow
location	outside, everywhere
frequency	sometimes, never, seldom

Slot Tests

One of the following slots will work in most cases.

> I did it _____ .
> I will do it _____ .
> I will _____ do it.

Unlike many other parts of speech, adverbs tend to have some degree of mobility. Although not all adverbs are mobile, if you find that a word can be moved to another position in a sentence with little or no change in meaning, it is probably an adverb.

She finished the job **slowly**.	She **slowly** finished the job.
Yesterday I saw *Rear Window.*	I saw *Rear Window* **yesterday**.

Closed Classes

A word class is closed if it is uncommon for new items to be added to it. This is certainly true of determiners, pronouns, prepositions, and the other classes listed below. It has been a very long time since English acquired any new prepositions, for example.

Closed class words vary in the amount of meaningful content they carry. Their main role is to help show the grammatical relationships between other words in a sentence, and sometimes to link words in one sentence to words and ideas that have been mentioned before. They are sometimes called *function words.*

Determiners

1. Articles

indefinite **(IndefArt)**	a (for nouns beginning with a consonant sound)
	a book, **a** year, **a** union
	an (for nouns beginning with a vowel sound)
	an egg, **an** uncle, **an** hour
definite **(DefArt)**	the

2. Demonstrative Determiners *(DemonD)*

Like other determiners, a demonstrative determiner refers to a noun that comes immediately or soon afterward.

this	**This** lesson is fascinating.
that	**That** long lesson was stimulating.
these	**These** easy lessons will thrill you.
those	**Those** lessons are over.

Notice that *this* and *these* are used to refer to nouns that are "near," in terms of space and time from the reference point of the speaker. *That* and *those* generally refer to things that are more remote in terms of space or time.

IMPORTANT: Don't confuse *DemonD* with demonstrative pronouns, which are described below.

3. Possessive Pronoun Determiners *(PossProD)*

Possessive pronoun determiners come from the *Personal Pronoun Paradigm* (see next section). Some textbooks call these *Possessive Pronouns,* but you should be careful not to confuse them with the *Independent Possessive Pronouns (IndPossPro).*

my	
your	
her	
his	All of these determiners typically precede a noun.
its	
our	
your	
their	

4. Interrogative Pro-Determiners *(IntProD)*

These determiners also typically precede a noun, and are used to form questions.

what	**What** magazine would you like to read?
which	**Which** university is the best in Canada?
whose	**Whose** office is this?

Pronouns

People often say that pronouns "take the place of nouns." Although that sometimes appears to be true, it often is not. For instance, consider this sentence:

Nobody came to Brian's party.

Although *nobody* is clearly a pronoun, it is not possible to identify any noun that it replaces. Rather than say that pronouns *replace* nouns, it is better to think of them as words that can have the same kinds of grammatical functions as nouns. For example, just like nouns they can serve as subjects and objects in sentences.

1. Personal Pronouns (Pro)

Quick Quiz: Complete the Personal Pronoun Chart Below					
Person	Subject Case (Pro)	Object Case (Pro)	Independent Possessive Pronouns (IndPossPro)	Reflexive Pronouns (Pro)	Possessive Pronoun Determiners (PossProD)
1st singular	I	me	mine	myself	my
2nd singular					
3rd singular					
1st plural					
2nd plural					
3rd plural					
2nd singular (archaic)					
2nd plural (dialectal)					
2nd plural (dialectal)					

REMINDER: The items in the last column above are not pronouns.

2. Indefinite Pronouns *(Pro)*

something	anything	everything	nothing
someone	anyone	everyone	no one
somebody	anybody	everybody	nobody

3. Interrogative Pronouns *(IntPro)*

who	**Who** has seen the wind?
whom (archaic)	**Whom** did you see?
what	**What** is the sound of one hand clapping?

4. Relative Pronouns *(RelPro)*

who	The man **who** won the election was ecstatic.
whom (archaic)	The woman **whom** we saw on TV was Joe's friend.
which	This shirt, **which** I bought at Rich's, is made of silk.
that	The country **that** the Prime Minister visited was China.

5. Demonstrative Pronouns *(DemonPro)*

Demonstrative pronouns should not be confused with demonstrative determiners. A demonstrative determiner modifies a noun, but a demonstrative pronoun stands in the place of a noun. Therefore, a demonstrative pronoun can be the subject or object (among other things) of a sentence.

this	**This** is a grammar lesson. I love **this**!
that	**That** is a fact.
these	**These** are examples of sentences with pronouns.
those	**Those** are fascinating.

Auxiliaries

Words in this class must be used with a verb. The verb may follow immediately or appear soon after the auxiliary.

1. HAVE, BE, DO *(Aux)*

HAVE	(have, has, had)
	Louise **has** just arrived.
BE	(be, am, are, is, was, were, been)
	Louise **is** working at the office today.
DO	(do, does, did, done)
	Do you need any rutabagas today?
	I **do**n't need any.
	You **do** complain too much! (emphatic)

2. Modals *(Modal)*

can	could
will	would
may	might
shall (archaic)	should
	must
	had better

3. Catenatives or Semi-modals *(Caten)*

These are "two-part" auxiliaries, all of which end with *to*. These auxiliaries are often contracted in spoken English, as shown in the second column.

have to	"hafta"
ought to	"otta"
want to	"wanna"
used to	"usta"
need to	
dare to	

Prepositions (Prep)

Prepositions introduce *prepositional phrases* with a wide range of meanings. The examples below are not exhaustive.

location	on (the wall), beside (the house), over (the fence)
time	at (six o'clock), on (Friday), after (the movie), before (dinner)
duration	for (two weeks)
instrument	with (a hammer), by (hand)
manner	with (pleasure), in (a hurry), like (a queen)
agency	by (Bill)
genitive	(Prime Minister) of (Canada)

Particles (Prt)

Particles often look like prepositions. However, they form a unit with a verb:

The demolitionist blew **up** the building.
The demolitionist blew the building **up**.

In the sentences above **blew up** is a two-word verb, and **up** is a particle.

Qualifiers (Qual)

Qualifiers can be said to qualify or intensify adjectives and adverbs. Although some textbooks treat qualifiers as adverbs, we will be careful to distinguish qualifiers from adverbs because of their special function.

very (old, quickly)
extremely (angry)
somewhat (pretty)
quite (busy)

Qualifiers have a fixed position—they precede the adjectives and adverbs they modify (see example (1) and the ungrammatical (2)), while adverbs can be placed in different positions in the sentence (see examples (3)–(6)).

1)	They are **extremely** busy.	Qual
2)	*__Extremely__ they are busy.	Qual
3)	**Fortunately**, we finished on time.	Adv
4)	We finished on time, **fortunately**.	Adv
5)	We **usually** finish on time.	Adv
6)	**Usually**, we finish on time.	Adv
7)	She is **absolutely** amazing.	Qual
8)	There's **absolutely** no food or open drinks in the classroom.	Qual

Note that "absolutely" in (8) precedes an NP!

Conjunctions

1. Coordinating Conjunctions *(CoordConj)*
   and
   or
   but
   nor
   so
   for
   yet

2. Subordinating Conjunctions *(SubConj)*
   because
   although
   while
   since
   so (under some circumstances) . . .

3. Correlative Conjunctions *(Correl)*
   either . . . or
   neither . . . nor
   if . . . then
   both . . . and

Others

1. Negative Marker "not" *(Neg)*
   Truth is **not** an easy thing to define.
   You ca**n't** take a goldfish for a walk. (contracted form)

2. Infinitive Marker "to" (No label)

> **To** err is human.
> Alan's great love is **to** play cards.

3. Expletive "there" *(Expl)*

> **There** is a hole in my tire.

4. Expletive "it" *(Expl)*

> **It** usually rains in December.
> **It** is easy to make potato salad.

5. Complementizer "that" *(COMP)*

> It is obvious **that** Bart is a brat.
> Bruce said **that** he would leave the door unlocked.

6. Miscellaneous cases

There are a number of less common types of words not covered in the sections above. Here are a few of them:

Interjections *(Interj)*

> Oh!
> Ouch!
> Darn! (euphemism)
> Shit! (vulgar)

Discourse particles *(DiscPrt)*

These words are often used when a speaker pauses while formulating an utterance or changes the topic of discussion.

> **Well** . . . I don't know what to say.
> **So**, what should we do for dinner?

Reaction signals *(RS)*

These are used in response to a prior question or remark.

> Were you at home on the night of April 12? . . . **Yes**.
> Are you asleep? . . . **No**.

Things You Need to Know About
Word Classes

A brief review of the traditional definitions of word classes focusing primarily on the meaning of words quickly reveals that meaning alone is an insufficient criterion to identify word classes. The following is a summary of the main points based on Crystal (1995), and Stewart and Vaillette (2001).

Traditional Definitions	Comments

NOUNS name people, things, and places. Examples: *doctor, book, Vancouver.*	■ This definition excludes many nouns which are not "persons, places, and things" such as:
	   ■ abstract notions like *loyalty, jealousy,* and *joy;*
	   ■ words with noun morphemes like *nothingness;*
	   ■ actions like *jump* in *"That was a great **jump** that you made."*
	 ■ Makes no reference to morphology or syntax.

VERBS are "doing words" or "action words." Examples: *play, do, draw.*	■ Excludes state verbs like *know, remember,* and *be.* ■ Cannot account for verbs like *resemble* and *have.* ■ Makes no reference to morphology or syntax.
ADJECTIVES modify or restrict the application of nouns by adding something to their meaning. Examples: *pretty, this, the.*	■ Allows a wide range of elements (e.g., *the, his, all*) that have different grammatical properties. ■ Does not exclude nouns or NPs in certain types of constructions (e.g., *Jim, my coworker*). ■ Makes no reference to morphology or syntax.
ADVERBS modify any part of speech except a noun or pronoun. Examples: *now, always, quickly, very.*	■ Some adverbs like *interestingly* can modify sentences, not parts of speech. ■ Does not account for the fact that words like *very* and *quite* have different properties from words like *usually* and *often.* ■ Makes no reference to morphology and syntax.

Open Classes (Content Words)

Things You Need to Know About
Word Classes

Traditional Definitions	Comments
PRONOUNS are used as nouns or noun-equivalents (i.e., act as nouns). Examples: *she, that, where, yours.*	■ The definition needs to be altered—pronouns are used instead of noun phrases, not just nouns (e.g., *she* refers to the whole phrase *the cute little girl,* not just the word *girl;* **the cute little she*). ■ Makes no reference to morphology or syntax.
PREPOSITIONS are placed before nouns or noun-equivalents to show in what relation the person or thing stands to something else. Examples: *in, from, for, in front of.*	■ This definition provides a clear syntactic criterion. ■ Prepositions go before noun phrases rather than just nouns. ■ Prepositions may also be used in other parts of the sentence; e.g., *This is the book I told you **about**.* ■ More than just persons and things are involved, (e.g., **in** *denial,* **about** *love*).
CONJUNCTIONS join words, phrases, or clauses together. Examples: *and, before, as soon as.*	■ This otherwise good definition is not restrictive enough; prepositions might also be said to have a joining function (e.g., *the book on the table*).
INTERJECTIONS are words or sounds thrown into a sentence to express the meaning of the mind. Examples: *Oh, Bravo!*	■ This definition is vague and needs to acknowledge that interjections do not enter into the construction of sentences.

Closed Classes (Function Words)

Things You Need to Know About

Word Classes

More Word Classes (syntactically distinctive from the above classes)	Comments Subcategories/Examples
DETERMINERS: words which can be used instead of *the* and *a* in the noun phrase, expressing such notions as quantity, number, possession, and definiteness (traditionally classified as adjectives). Examples: *some, much, that, my.*	■ **ARTICLES:** definite article *the* (***the*** *horse*) and indefinite article *a/an* (***a*** *horse,* ***an*** *egg*). ■ **DEMONSTRATIVE DETERMINERS:** *this, that, these, those* (***These*** *courses are difficult.*). **Note:** do **not** confuse demonstrative determiners above with demonstrative pronouns; e.g., ***This*** *is a hit. I love* ***this***! ■ **POSSESSIVE PRONOUN DETERMINERS:** *my, your* (***my*** *book*) ■ **GENITIVES:** e.g., ***Leo's*** *book* ■ **INTERROGATIVE PRO-DETERMINERS:** *what, which, whose* (e.g., ***Which*** *magazine would you like to read?*)
CONJUNCTS: A group of words whose function is to relate (or 'conjoin') independent grammatical units such as clauses, sentences, or paragraphs. Traditional grammars call them conjunctive adverbs.	■ Examples: *however, meanwhile, otherwise, namely.*
AUXILIARIES: a group of words whose function is to assist the head of a verb phrase in a clause to express several basic grammatical contrasts, such as of person, number, and tense. Traditional grammars sometimes recognized these as a separate class of 'defective verbs.'	■ **Have, be, do, get** (*Ben* ***has*** *arrived; Ben* ***is*** *telecommuting today;* ***Do*** *you need anything?; We* ***got*** *robbed = We* ***were*** *robbed* in North American English). ■ **Modals:** *can, may, would, should,* etc. ■ **Catenatives (Semi-modals):** *have to, ought to, need to, want to, used to, be able to, be going to,* etc.
PARTICLES: they look like prepositions and form a unit with the verb.	■ Examples: *He made* ***up*** *the story. He made the story* ***up***.
OTHER: ■ negative marker *not* ■ infinitive marker *to* ■ expletive *there* ■ expletive *it* ■ complementizer *that* ■ interjections ■ discourse particles ■ reaction signals	■ *This is* ***not*** *true.* ■ *It's hard* ***to*** *tell.* ■ ***There*** *is someone in the house.* ■ ***It's*** *hot outside.* ■ *I know* ***that*** *he's here.* ■ ***Ouch!*** ***Darn!*** ■ *He is,* ***like***, *a good guy,* ***you know***. ■ *Are you still there?* ***Yes***.

More Closed Classes (Function Words)

Useful Tests for Word Classes

Nouns

1) _____ + plural morpheme[1]   (song-song**s**)
2) Determiner _____   (the song)
3) Determiner Adjective _____   (this nice song)

[1]Only with countable nouns; e.g., song-song**s** *child-child**ren***, *wom**a**n-wom**e**n*, but **not** with uncountable nouns such as *happiness—*happinesses*.

Verbs

1) _____ + tense morpheme   (walk-**walked**)
2) _____ + third person singular morpheme   (walk-**walks**)
3) _____ + progressive morpheme   (**is walking**)
4) Auxiliary _____   (can **walk**)
5) _____!   (**walk**! [imperative])

Adjectives

1) _____ + er/est   (**nice**, **nicer**, **nicest**), or
more/most[2] _____   (more/most **interesting**)
3) Determiner _____ Noun   (this **nice** lady)
4) Linking verb _____   (This lady seems **nice**)
5) Qualifier _____   (unexpectedly **nice**)

[2]Note that "more" and "most" are independent word versions of the morphemes "-er" and "-est." When used with adjectives and adverbs, they behave like Qualifiers. However, they can also be used with nouns; e.g., "more students," in which case we can parse them as general determiners **(Det).**

Adverbs

1) [Adjective + ly]Adverb[3]   (**eagerly**, **skillfully**)
2) _____ Verb or Verb Phrase   (**quietly** entered the room)
or Verb/VP _____   (moved **carefully**)
3) more/most[4] _____   (more/most **interestingly**)
_____ + er/est   (**faster**)
4) Adverbs may occur in several positions in a sentence:

a) *Cautiously, they stepped onto the slippery sidewalk.*
b) *They cautiously stepped onto the slippery sidewalk.*
c) *They stepped cautiously onto the slippery sidewalk.*
d) *They stepped onto the slippery sidewalk cautiously.*

[3]Does **not** apply to all adverbs; e.g., *fast*.

[4]With some adverbs only.

Determiners

1) _____ (Adjective) Noun   (**the** small things; **many** small things)

Auxiliary Verbs

1) Noun phrase _____ Verb phrase   (I **might** go; I **have** gone)
2) _____ Noun phrase Verb phrase?   (**Did** I go?)
3) _____ not   (I **might** not go)

Prepositions

1) _____ Noun phrase   (**in** the bag)
2) right _____ Noun phrase[5]   (right **into** the store)

[5] With some prepositions only

Conjunctions

1) Noun _____ Noun   (mom **and** dad)
2) Adjective _____ Adjective   (delicious **but** unhealthy)
3) NP _____ NP   (a young boy **and** an older girl)
4) Adj phrase _____ Adj phrase   (unusually slim **and** unexpectedly clumsy)
5) Sentence _____ Sentence   (He will leave now **or** he will stay forever.)

Pronouns[6]

1) Can be subjects   (**I** am here)
2) Can be objects   (Dana saw **me**)

[6] Note that Possessive forms like *his, my,* and *her* are determiners (see above), not pronouns.

Qualifiers

1) _____ Adjective   (**unusually** old)
2) _____ Adv   (he walked **unusually** slowly)

Meaning & Form, Syntactic Environment, and Syntactic Function

For many word classes, in addition to meaning, form, and the syntactic environment in which words occur (e.g., words to the left or to the right), we need to consider their syntactic function.

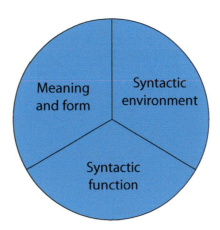

Nouns and Noun Phrase Functions

One of the most useful criteria in identifying nouns, for example, is the fact that nouns and the noun phrases **(NPs)** they belong to can function as Subjects **(Subj),** Direct Objects **(DO),** Indirect Objects **(IO),** Predicate Nouns **(PredN),** Object Complements **(OC),** or Objects of Prepositions **(Obj/Prep).**

A noun phrase can consist of a single element—a noun or a pronoun (e.g., students, they), or it can also include determiners and modifiers (e.g., the best students).

Syntactic Functions of Nouns and NPs		Examples
1. Subjects	Subj	**1.** **Dogs** are good friends.
2. Direct Objects	DO	**2.** We heard **dogs.**
3. Indirect Objects	IO	**3.** We gave **the dogs** treats.
4. Predicate Nouns	PredN	**4.** These are **smart dogs.**
5. Object Complements	OC	**5.** We call our friends **dogs.**
6. Objects of Prepositions	Obj/Prep	**6.** We were talking about **dogs.**

Some words can have more than one function, and therefore can belong to more than one word class. Apart from obvious examples like *promise* (verb) and *promise* (noun), it is particularly helpful to identify the syntactic environment and functions of words which have identical forms such as "be" as the main verb (BE) and "be" as an auxiliary verb (Aux), some adjectives and adverbs, many prepositions and verbal particles, and some prepositions and conjunctions.

"be" as the Main Verb (BE) and "be" as an Auxiliary Verb (Aux)	Examples
1. "be" as the Main Verb (BE)	**1.** She has **been** a student since 2004. She **is** polite. She is **being** silly. She will **be** in the office by 8 o'clock.
2. "be" as an Auxiliary Verb (Aux)	**2.** He has **been** playing the piano for 5 years. He **was** playing the piano when you called. He **is** being silly.

Adjectives and Adverbs	Examples
1. Attributive Adjectives Predicate Adjectives	**1.** She has a **fast** car. **2.** She's done with the test. She is **fast**. **3.** She's not done with the test. She is **slow.**
2. Adverbs	**4.** He drives **fast.** **5.** He drives **slowly.** **6.** He drives **slow.** (informal)

Prepositions and Particles	Examples
1. Prepositions	**1.** They walked **down** the street. **2.** They came **up** the stairs. **3.** They came **with** their baby.
2. Verbal Particles	**4.** They calmed **down** the baby. They calmed the baby **down**. **5.** They came **up with** a great idea.

Prepositions and Conjunctions	Examples
1. Prepositions (+ NPs)	**1.** They called **after** the party.
2. Conjunctions (+ Clauses/Sentences)	**2.** **After** they bought the house, they stopped coming.

Determiners (determine nouns)	Pronouns (replace nouns)
1. Demonstrative Determiners **Example:** **This** lesson is boring.	**1.** Demonstrative Pronouns **Example:** **This** is boring.
2. Possessive Pro-Determiners **Example:** **My** bag is on the floor.	**2.** Possessive Pronouns **Example:** This bag is **mine.**
3. Interrogative Pro-Determiners **Example:** **What** colour is this?	**3.** Interrogative Pronouns **Example:** **What** is this?

Exercises

1. Which of the following words and expressions can be used as nouns or noun phrases? *Hint: Try using the words in actual sentences.*

   a) a notebook _____

   b) Vancouver _____

   c) smile _____

   d) the privileged _____

   e) swimming _____

   f) Starbucks _____

   g) 1998 _____

   h) a cry _____

   i) to love _____

   j) Joann McDonald _____

   k) my bad _____

   l) an Einstein _____

   m) round _____

2. Use the following four features of nouns as tests (features based on Crystal 1995:207), and try to answer the question "How noun-like is '*Beethoven*'? as compared to a noun like '*friendship*'?"

a) Nouns are words which can be the head of a noun phrase.

b) They are words which can be the subject of a clause.

c) They are words which can have a plural form.

d) They are words which display a suffix such as *-tion, -hood,* etc.

'friendship'

a) _____

b) _____

c) _____

d) _____

'Beethoven'

a) _____

b) _____

c) _____

d) _____

3. Identify the lexical category of the underlined words in the following sentences/phrases:

a) They **should** have called us **earlier**.   _____   _____

b) The boy ran **down** the street barefoot.   _____

c) We bought a new tablecloth for the **round** table.   _____

d) **Would** you spell your name for me, please?   _____

e) **This** is a **very** unusual name.   _____   _____

f) They returned **our** essays on **Friday**.   _____   _____

g) I **won't** **ask** you **to** go **to** that restaurant again.   _____   _____

   _____   _____

h) **It** is difficult to learn a foreign language, **but** it's a rewarding experience.   _____   _____

i) **Never** say "**never**."   _____   _____

j) **Which** book did you choose?   _____

k) **Which** is your favourite book?   _____

41

Answers to Exercises

1. All of these can be nouns/NPs:

a)	a notebook	I don't have a notebook.
b)	Vancouver	They moved to Vancouver in 1975.
c)	smile	The baby gave me a happy smile.
d)	the privileged	The privileged take many things for granted.
e)	swimming	Swimming is favourite pastime in the city.
f)	Starbucks	I don't know where the nearest Starbucks is.
g)	1998	1998 was a difficult year for the city.
h)	a cry	We heard a cry.
i)	to love	To love is easy.
j)	Joann McDonald	Joann McDonald is the executive manager of the society.
k)	my bad	My bad!
l)	an Einstein	He is quite smart but he is not an Einstein.
m)	round	The third round turned out to be difficult.

2. *'Friendship'* is an excellent noun because it satisfies all four criteria.

a) Nouns are words which can be the head of a noun phrase.
b) They are words which can be the subject of a clause.
c) They are words which can have a plural form.
d) They are words which display a suffix such as *-tion, -hood,* etc.

> **a)** *I highly value their friendship.*
> **b)** *Friendship is what matters to me most.*
> **c)** *This business rivalry ended many friendships.*
> **d)** *Friend**ship***

'Beethoven' is a much less typical noun.

a) Unlikely (except when it becomes a common noun; e.g., "This child is like a little Beethoven.").
b) Beethoven is one of the greatest composers of all time.
c) Unlikely (except in special cases; e.g., "They believe they've discovered two new Beethovens among these talented kids.").
d) None

3.
 a) They **should** have called us **earlier**.   Modal (should); Adv (earlier)
 b) The boy ran **down** the street barefoot.   Prep (down)
 c) We bought a new tablecloth for the **round** table.   Adj (round)
 d) **Would** you spell your name for me, please?   Modal (would)
 e) **This** is a **very** unusual name.   DemonPro (this); Qual (very)
 f) They returned **our** essays on **Friday**.   PossProD (our); PropN (Friday)
 g) I **won't** **ask** you **to** go **to** that restaurant again.   Modal+Neg (won't); Vg (ask);
                  Infinitive Marker (to); Prep (to)

 h) **It** is difficult to learn a foreign language, **but**   Expl (it); CoordConj (but)
    it's a rewarding experience.
 i) **Never** say "**never**".   Adv (never); N ("never")
 j) **Which** book did you choose?   IntProD (which)
                 [determines the noun "book"]
 k) **Which** is your favourite book?   IntPro

Inflectional and Derivational Affixes

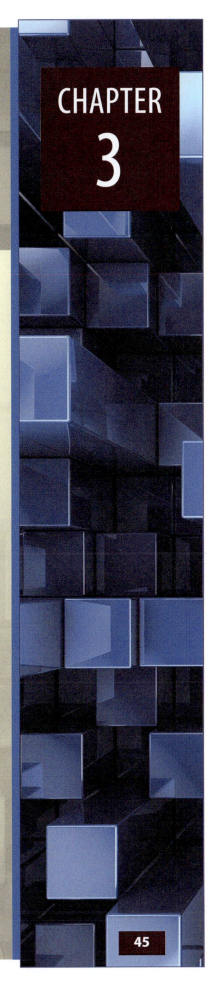

In this section we will consider labels that can be used to describe the structure of words themselves. Notice that these are *not* parsing labels, and we will not be using them when we parse sentences.

Inflectional Markers

English has eight inflectional affixes that all appear as suffixes. Adding an inflectional affix to a word does not change its part of speech; nor does it create a "new word." Rather, inflections are used as a grammatical device to mark things like number (for nouns) and person or tense (for verbs). If you find that an affix does not fit one of the eight types below, you can conclude that it is *not* an inflectional affix.

Noun Inflections

1. Plural Marker *(-Plur)*
Most nouns can be pluralized, usually by adding '-s' or '-es.'

cat	cats
parsnip	parsnips
box	boxes

Irregular nouns form the plural in some other way.

child	children
mouse	mice
deer	deer
man	men

2. Genitive Marker *(-Gen)*
The genitive of singular nouns is usually spelled by adding an apostrophe + 's.'

Jack's pencil
the cat's tail
the student's grades (one student)

Genitives of regular plural nouns are commonly spelled by adding 's' + an apostrophe.

the students' grades (more than one student)
her parents' house (it belongs to both parents)

The genitive is used to indicate a relationship between two nouns. Often this is a "possessive" relationship, but there are several other possibilities.

Quick Quiz

See whether you can describe the meaning of the genitive in each case below. Are any of the phrases ambiguous?

Jane's bike   _____

Jane's hair   _____

Jane's grades   _____

Jane's mother   _____

Jane's hometown   _____

Jane's job   _____

Jane's book   _____

Jane's intelligence   _____

Jane's reputation   _____

Verb Inflections

3. Third Person Singular Marker *(-3PS)*
This suffix is added to verbs in the present tense when the subject represents the third person singular. It is usually spelled as '-s' or '-es.'

(he, she, it, Mary) work<u>s</u>
(he, she, it, Mary) go<u>es</u>

A few verbs have irregular 3PS forms.

be	is
have	has
do	does

4. The Present Participle Suffix *(-ing)*
This present participle verb form has a variety of functions that will be discussed later in the course.

work	working
be	being
drive	driving

5. The Past Tense Marker *(-Past)*
The regular past tense is usually spelled by adding '-d' or '-ed' to a verb.

work	worked
live	lived
wait	waited

A number of verbs and auxiliaries have irregular past tense forms

Verb	**Past Tense Form**
be	was, were
have	had
do	did
eat	ate
write	wrote
drive	drove

6. Past Participle Marker *(-PastPart)*
You can determine the past participle of a verb by identifying the form that occurs after 'have' in a sentence frame such as "I have _____ ."

Regular past participles look identical to regular past tense forms (i.e., they are spelled by adding '-d' or '-ed'), but they function differently.

(I have) work**ed**.
(I have) live**d**.
(I have) wait**ed**.

Irregular past participles are often different from past tense forms and may be formed in various ways.

Verb	Past Tense Form	Past Participle Form
be	was, were	been
have	had	had
do	did	done
eat	ate	eaten
write	wrote	written
drive	drove	driven

Adjective and Adverb Inflections

7. Comparative Marker *(-Compar)*

The comparative forms of many adjectives and adverbs are created by adding '-er,' sometimes with minor spelling modifications.

old	older
tall	taller
busy	busier
fast	faster

8. Superlative Marker *(-Superl)*

The superlative forms of adjectives and adverbs are typically created by adding '-est.'

old	oldest
tall	tallest
busy	busiest
fast	fastest

NOTE: A few adjectives and adverbs have irregular comparative and superlative forms.

Basic Form	Comparative	Superlative
good	better	best
bad	worse	worst

Some adjectives and adverbs (especially those of more than two syllables) have **periphrastic** comparative and superlative forms. These require the qualifiers 'more' and 'most.'

beautiful	more beautiful	most beautiful
intelligent	more intelligent	most intelligent

Derivational Affixes

Derivational prefixes and suffixes are used to derive new words. Adding a derivational affix to a word will often (but not always) change its part of speech. English has hundreds of derivational affixes. Some are highly productive (i.e., used in many words), while others are not. A few examples are given here. Note that these affixes may be analyzed in terms of the types of words they create, the types of words they may be added to, and the kinds of meanings they indicate.

Suffixes that derive new nouns:

-ity   generosity, sanity
-ant   inhabitant, servant

Suffixes that derive new verbs:

-ize   revolutionize, legalize
-ify   simplify, pacify

Suffixes that derive new adjectives:

-ous   courteous, bulbous
-ive   attractive, effective

Suffixes that derive new adverbs:

-ly   happily, quickly
-ward   backward

Agentive suffix (don't confuse with the comparative inflection):

-er   baker, worker

Diminutive suffixes:

-let   piglet, starlet
-ette   novelette, statuette

Reversative prefix (attaches to verbs):

un-   undo, untie

Negative prefix (attaches to adjectives and adverbs):

un-   unattractive, unusually

Degree prefixes:

super-   supernatural, supermarket
sub-   subordinate, subhuman

Negative prefix (attaches to verbs and adjectives):

dis-   distrust, disallow, disobey, dishonest, disrespectful

Repetitive prefix:

re-   rewrite, redo, recreate

Things You Need to Know About

Inflectional and Derivational Affixes

Affixes can be very useful when you are guessing the meaning of words, and when you are identifying parts of speech. However, there are some exceptions and false friends, which you need to keep in mind.

Affixes and the Meaning of Words	Exceptions and False Friends
(1) The **prefix "super-"** is added to words such as "size" and "car" to form "supersize" and "supercar," meaning "(making or being) extremely large/advanced/powerful, etc."	**(1)** Words like "superfluous" (meaning "unnecessary") cannot be derived in this way because "fluous" is not a word.
(2) Words containing the **prefix "re-"**, such as "reorganize" or "reproduce," usually mean "do something again or anew."	**(2)** Words like **real, read, reach, rely, render, rest** do not contain this prefix.
(3) Words with the **prefix "sub-"** often mean "under" (literally or metaphorically); e.g., submarine.	**(3)** "Sublime" means "majestic, supreme."
(4) Words ending in the **suffix "-able,"** such as "comparable" or "gradable," mean "able to do something or allowing something to be done."	**(4)** Some words ending in "-able" do not contain the suffix "-able" and/or do not display this meaning; e.g., **"table, cable, stable, constable,"** etc.
(5) Add your own example(s) here.	**(5)** Find out if your example(s) has (have) exceptions.

Affixes and Parts of Speech	Exceptions and False Friends
(1) The **prefix "un-":** **(i)** reverses the meaning of verbs; e.g., "untie, unpack, unbuckle," etc. **(ii)** creates the opposite meaning in adjectives and adverbs; e.g., "unborn, unreal, uneducated, unusually," etc.	**(1)** **(a)** Some words with this prefix are neither adjectives, nor adverbs, nor verbs; e.g., **"unease"** and **"the untouchable"** are nouns, while **"unlike"** is a preposition"; **(b)** Words like **"uniform"** and **"unilateral"** contain a different **prefix, "uni-",** meaning "one."
(2) Words ending in the **suffix "-tion"** such as "registration" and "creation," are usually nouns.	**(2)** Words like **"position, station, question, mention,"** etc. can be verbs too.
(3) Words ending in the **suffix "-s(s)ion"** such as "television, decision, regression" are usually nouns.	**(3)** Words like **"envision"** and **"commission,"** can be verbs too.
(4) Word ending in the **suffix "-ly";** e.g., "responsibly" and "typically," are usually adverbs.	**(4)** A number of adjectives also end in "-ly"; e.g., **"lovely, friendly, manly, womanly, slovenly, likely,"** etc.
(5) Add your own example here.	**(5)** Find out if your example has exceptions.

Exercises for Sections 2 and 3
Identifying Parts of Speech and Inflectional Markers

A. Parse each sentence by writing the appropriate labels on the line below. Use ONLY the following labels for the parts of speech:

N, GenN, PropN, Pro, DemonPro, IndPossPro, IndefArt, DefArt, DemonD, PossProD, Aux, Modal, Caten, V, Prt, Adj, Adv, Qual, Prep, CoordConj, Neg, Expl
 REMINDER: Note that *-Plur, -Gen, -3PS, -ing, -Past, -PastPart, -Compar, -Superl are not parsing labels. We will **not** use these symbols when parsing sentences in the other exercises.*

1. January is the rainiest month.

_____

2. I'll see you after the office party.

_____

3. I really have to leave now.

_____

4. I wish you'd leave your window open.

_____

5. The slithy toves did gyre and gimbel in the wabe.

_____

6. That is the best vegetable soup I've ever tasted.

_____

7. It looks like a Picasso, but no one is completely sure.

_____

8. That cat has a sore leg.

_____

9. The bear has been catching fish and eating them.

_____

10. It's damn cold in Prince George this week.

_____

11. I called him up, but he wasn't there.

_____

12. Tony broke Rose's plate and felt very bad about it.

_____

13. She's hardly started work.

_____

14. I see you lost your pencil. Do you want to use mine?

_____

15. Despite the rain, we went for a walk in Queen Elizabeth Park.

_____

B. How many different ways can each of the words below be used? Give a sentence illustrating each different use.

    e.g., **just**   Adj: She's a **just** person.
            Adv: She has **just** left.

 1. will

_____

_____

 2. well

_____

_____

 3. light

_____

_____

4. way

_____

_____

5. wrong

_____

_____

6. pretty

_____

_____

C. Identify all the inflectional markers in the sentences below using the following inflectional labels:

-Plur, -Gen, -3PS, -ing, -Past, -PastPart, -Compar, -Superl

1. She's nearly completed the project.

2. It's time for Karen to analyze her data.

3. Joan's friends are coming over later.

4. The weather is more pleasant than we had expected.

5. Ralph's a worldly person.

6. The mice's tails have been cut off.

D. Identify the part of speech of the underlined words in the following sentences.

Hint: Use a combination of ways to identify parts of speech: word meaning, word form, syntactic environment, and syntactic function.

1. <u>This</u> makes quinoa an excellent option for vegetarians, vegans, and anyone interested in adding non-meat proteins to their diet.
[from "How to Make quinoa . . . ," yahoo.com]

_____

_____

2. I wish you and **yours** a safe and happy holiday season.

_____

_____

3. Everyone has a **favourite**.

_____

_____

4. The two biggest upcoming trends everyone has been looking at are **virtualization** and cloud-computing.
[from "Death of the PC . . . ," thevarguy.com]

_____

_____

5. Both of these technologies, which in some ways **complement** each other, do not rely on traditional 'PCs.'
[from "Death of the PC . . . ," thevarguy.com]

_____

_____

6. Those Christmas ornaments are really great **finds** in Vienna.

_____

_____

7. SFU president Andrew Petter **guests** on the "Your Education Matters" program on Shaw-TV (Cable 4).
[from the SFU website, sfu.ca]

_____

_____

8. Thank you, Don! Love you **lots**.

_____

_____

9. All persons making deliveries and **pick-ups** should go to the main mailroom.
[from "Hand Deliveries . . . ," sec.gov]

_____

_____

10. The paper towel "Bounty" is known as the "**Quicker Picker Upper**" because of its speed and effectiveness in blotting up a liquid spill.
[adapted from "The Quicker Picker Upper Experiment," pubs.acs.org]

_____

_____

11. The paper towel "Bounty" is known as the "Quicker Picker Upper" because of its speed and effectiveness in blotting up a liquid **spill.**
[adapted from "The Quicker Picker Upper Experiment," pubs.acs.org]

_____

_____

12. This was **way** too easy!

_____

_____

13. Use Facebook to get free stuff. See how you can **social-network** your way into free samples and more.
[from a Facebook commercial]

_____

_____

14. **Together** is amazing.
[from a Shaw commercial]

_____

_____

15. I'm sitting **pretty** these days.
[from an H & R Block radio commercial]

_____

_____

16. We're all **Canucked out** today.
[Father with a young boy all dressed up in Canucks outfits talking to a bank clerk, March, 2011]

_____

_____

Answers to Selected Exercises

A. **1.** January is the rainiest month.
PropN   V   DefArt   Adj   N

2. I'll see you after the office party.
Pro+Modal   V   Pro   Prep   DefArt   N   N

3. I really have to leave now.
Pro   Adv   Caten (2 wds)   V   Adv

4. I wish you'd leave your window open.
Pro   V   Pro+Modal   V   PossProD   N   Adj

5. **The slithy toves did gyre and gimbel in the wabe.**
DefArt   Adj   N   Aux   V   CoordConj   V   Prep   DefArt   N
or   V   N   and   N

6. That is the best vegetable soup I've ever tasted.
DemonPro   V   DefArt   Adj   N   N   Pro+Aux   Adv   V

7. It looks like a Picasso, but no one is
Pro   V   Prep   IndefArt   PropN   CoordConj   Pro (2wds)   V
completely sure.
Qual   Adj

8. That cat has a sore leg.
DemonD   N   V   IndefArt   Adj   N

9. The bear has been catching fish and eating them.
DefArt   N   Aux   Aux   V   N   CoordConj   V   Pro

10. It's damn cold in Prince George this week.
Expl+V   Qual   Adj   Prep   PropN (2 wds)   DemonD   N

11.

I	called	him	up,	but		he	wasn't	there.
Pro	V	Pro	Prt	CoordConj		Pro	V+Neg	Adv

12.

Tony	broke	**Rose's**	plate	and		felt	very	bad	about	it.
PropN	V	**GenN**	N	CoordConj		V	Qual	Adj	Prep	Pro

13.

She's	hardly	started	work.
Pro+Aux	Adv	V	N

14.

I	see	you	lost	your	pencil.	Do	you	want to	use	mine?
Pro	V	Pro	V	PossProD	N	Aux	Pro	Caten (2 wds)	V	IndPossPro

15.

Despite		the	rain	we	went	for	a	walk	in
Prep		DefArt	N	Pro	V	Prep	IndefArt	N	Prep

Queen Elizabeth Park.
PropN (3 wds)

D.

1. DemonPro	6. N	12. Qual
2. N (similar to "your family"; DO)	7. V	13. V
	8. Adv	14. N
3. N (DO of V "has")	9. N	15. Adv (or Adj:Adv)
4. N	10. PropN	16. Adj (similar to "we're dressed up/decked out in Canucks outfits")
5. V	11. N	

Verb Types, Multi-Word Verbs, and Related Constituency Issues

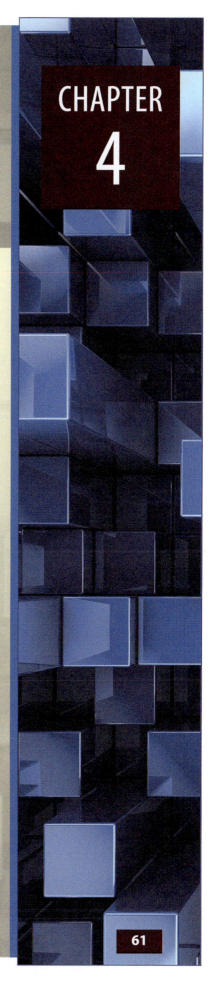

Verb Types

There are many classifications of English verbs, but from a learnability point of view, and for the purposes of conducting basic analysis of English sentences, we find the following six categories of verbs in English particularly helpful (based on Morenberg 2010):

1) Intransitive verbs **(VI)**
2) Linking verbs **(VL)**
3) Transitive verbs **(VT)**
4) Verbs like "give" **(Vg)** [pronounced "Vee Gee"]
5) Verbs like "consider" **(Vc)** [pronounced like "Vee See"]
6) The Verb **BE**

1) **Intransitive Verbs (VI)** do not normally require any complements; their meaning is complete without any additional words in the VP:Predicate (rare exceptions will be noted as we come across them), and they could be the last word in the sentence; e.g.,

> The bus **arrived.**
> The man **stopped.**
> They **ran.**

However, it is not a requirement for a VI to be the last word in the sentence. VI verbs can be accompanied by a number of adverbs, specifying the time, place, manner, etc. in which the event takes place.

> The bus **arrived at 3 o'clock**.
> **Suddenly**, the man **stopped in the middle of the street**.
> They **ran fast through the forest**.

2) **Linking Verbs (VL)** link the NP:Subject on the left side of the verb and a Predicate form on the right side of the verb in declarative

sentences. The predicate form is either (a) an NP, called a Predicate Noun or Nominative (**PredN**), which renames the subject; or (b) an AdjP, called a Predicate Adjective (**PredAdj**), which provides some qualities or characteristic features of the subject. Unlike intransitive verbs, but like all other verb types, linking verbs **cannot** be the last word in statements, and their meaning is not complete without their complement as the sentences marked with an asterisk indicate (Note that some of these sentences may be grammatical in other contexts; i.e., when these verbs are used as VI verbs).

a) She **remained president**$_{[PredN]}$ for three more years.
*She remained.
He **turned traitor**$_{[PredN]}$.
*He turned.

b) She **remained honest**$_{[PredAdj]}$.
The leaves **turned brown**$_{[PredAdj]}$.
*The leaves turned.

3) **Transitive Verbs (VT)** require an NP functioning as a direct object (**DO**) on the right side of the verb in statements; otherwise, their meaning is incomplete (see the ungrammatical sentences below). The NP:DO usually introduces an entity which is being acted upon, or is affected in some way by the subject.

They **created an empire**$_{[DO]}$.
*They **created**.
The parents **are building a new playground**$_{[DO]}$.
*The parents **are building**.
I **recognized him**$_{[DO]}$.
*I recognized.

Sentences which contain VT verbs can be turned into passive structures in the following ways:

- the NP:DO of the active sentence becomes the NP:Subject of the passive sentence, also called **Grammatical Subject;**
- the verb is turned into a passive verb with the help of the Auxiliary verb BE and the past participle form of the verb (e.g., the active verb "see" becomes passive "is/are seen");
- the NP:Subject of the active sentence may optionally occur in a prepositional phrase (PP) with the Prep "by", also called **Logical Subject** (because it continues to be the entity that does the action).

Notice that the verb in the passive structure remains transitive, although the DO is not in its usual place on the right side of the verb (the DO has become the Subject, and now precedes the verb).

Active	They$_{[Subj]}$ **created an empire**$_{[DO]}$.
Passive	An empire$_{[Subj]}$ **was created** (by **them**$_{[Obj/Prep]}$).
Active	The parents$_{[Subj]}$ **are building a new playground**$_{[DO]}$.
Passive	A new playground$_{[Subj]}$ **is being built** (by **the parents**$_{[Obj/Prep]}$).

There are a few exceptions when VT verbs cannot be made passive
(a) when the NP:DO is a reflexive pronoun (e.g., "themselves"), and
(b) when the VT verbs are "have," "weigh," "cost," or "resemble."

- **a)** He <u>**saw himself**</u>[DO] in the mirror.
  *Himself <u>**was seen**</u> in the mirror (by him).
- **b)** I <u>**have a car**</u>[DO].
  *A car <u>**is had**</u> (by me).
  This piano <u>**weighs a ton**</u>[DO].
  *A ton <u>**is weighed**</u> (by this piano).

4) Vg Verbs are called this because they behave like the verb "give" in many ways. Like transitive verbs, they require an NP:DO, but unlike transitive verbs, they require another NP complement called Indirect Object **(IO)**. For this reason, they are sometimes called ditransitive verbs. So, an active sentence with a Vg verb includes a minimum of three different entities (except when a reflexive pronoun is the DO) expressed by three different NPs:

- **(i)** the NP:Subject, or the giver,
- **(ii)** the NP:DO, an entity (usually an object) that transfers property literally or metaphorically from the NP:Subject to the NP:IO, and
- **(iii)** an NP:IO, or the receiver, a usually animate entity receiving the object. The IO may precede the DO, or it may follow the DO, in which case it is introduced by the Preposition **"to"** or **"for,"** but both objects are required by the verb, otherwise the result is ungrammaticality or a different meaning.

I[Subj] <u>**gave my brother**</u>[IO] <u>**the picture**</u>[DO].
I[Subj] <u>**gave the picture**</u>[DO] to <u>**my brother**</u>[IO].
*I[Subj] <u>**gave the picture**</u>[DO].
*I[Subj] <u>**gave**</u> to <u>**my brother**</u>[IO].
I[Subj] <u>**bought my brother**</u>[IO] <u>**a camera**</u>[DO].
I[Sub] <u>**bought a camera**</u>[DO] for <u>**my brother**</u>[IO].
*I[Subj] <u>**bought my brother**</u>.
I[Subj] <u>**bought a camera**</u>[DO].   [VT not Vg verb, different meaning]

Like sentences with transitive verbs, sentences which contain Vg verbs can be turned into passive structures, with either object having the ability to become the subject in the passive structure. Again, if the doer of the action is mentioned in the passive, it is introduced by the preposition "by," so it's the object of the preposition "by" and Logical Subject.

Active   I <u>**gave my brother**</u>[IO] <u>**the picture**</u>[DO].
Passive   The picture[Subj] <u>**was given**</u> to <u>**my brother**</u>[IO] (by <u>**me**</u>[Obj/Prep]).
              My brother[Subj] <u>**was given the picture**</u>[DO] (by <u>**me**</u>[Obj/Prep]).

Similar to sentences with VT verbs, when the NP:DO is a reflexive pronoun, the passive structure is ungrammatical.

Active   They[Subj] <u>**gave themselves**</u>[IO] <u>**a round of applause**</u>[DO].
Passive   *Themselves <u>**were given**</u> a round of applause (by them).

5) Vc Verbs are called this because many of them behave like the verb "consider." Like Vg verbs, they require two complements, one of which is NP:DO. The second complement, called an Object Complement **(OC)**, completes the meaning of the DO and is necessary for the meaning of the Vc to be complete. The OC can be one of three types:

a) a noun phrase (NP:OC),

b) an adjective phrase (AdjP:OC), or

c) an infinitive phrase (InfP:OC). Without any of these complements, the sentence is either ungrammatical or has a different meaning. In sentence (a), for example, I am not simply considering my brother; I consider him to be a hero.

a) I **consider my brother**[DO] a hero[NP:OC].
   *I **consider my brother**.
   *I **consider** a hero.

b) I **consider my brother**[DO] famous[AdjP:OC].
   *I **consider my brother**.
   *I **consider** famous.

c) I **consider my brother**[DO] to be my best friend[InfP:OC].
   *I **consider my brother**.
   *I **consider** to be my best friend.

Like sentences with transitive and Vg verbs, sentences with Vc verbs can be turned into passive structures. Only the DO of the Vc can become the subject in the passive structure. Again, if the doer of the action is mentioned in the passive, it is introduced by the preposition "by," so it's the object of the preposition "by," and Logical Subject and if the DO is a reflexive pronoun, the passive is not grammatical.

Active	Many people **consider him**[DO] **a hero**[NP:OC].
Passive	He[Subj] **is considered a hero**[NP:OC] (by **many people**[Obj/Prep]).
Active	He **considers himself**[DO] **a hero**[NP:OC].
Passive	*Himself **is considered a hero** (by **him**).

6) The Verb BE is the only member in this category. Like linking verbs, it links the NP:Subject on the left side of the verb and a Predicate form on the right side of the verb in declarative sentences. The predicate form can be:

a) an NP which functions as a Predicate Noun/Nominative (PredN), and renames the subject; or

b) an AdjP, which functions as a Predicate Adjective (PredAdj), and provides some qualities or characteristic features of the subject; or

c) an AdvP called Predicate Adverb **(PredAdv)**, which usually provides the location of the subject; the PredAdv can be an adverb; e.g., "here," or a PP; e.g., "at home."

The meaning of the verb BE is not complete without its complement (see the sentences marked with an asterisk as ungrammatical).

a) She **is the president**[PredN].
   *She is.

b)   She **is honest**[PredAdj].
   *She is.

c)   She **is in the office**[PredAdv].
   *She is.

The ability of the verb BE to take a PredAdv as a complement (as in (c))
distinguishes it from linking verbs, because although VL verbs could be
modified by optional adverbs (e.g., *He remained honest **for the rest of his
life***), these adverbs must occur in conjunction with a PredN or a PredAdj.
Thus **He remained for the rest of his life,* where the intended meaning is
that of a VL, is ungrammatical without the predicate form *honest* (note,
however, that the same verb could be used as a VI; e.g., *I left*[VI] *the small
town when I was 18, but he remained*[VI] *for the rest of his life*).

Multi-Word Verbs

Multi-word or "phrasal" verbs are combinations of verbs and particles **(Prt)** that function together as constituents. They tend to have idiomatic meanings that cannot be
easily predicted by considering the meanings of the words they comprise. Consider,
for example, the differences in meaning conveyed by these expressions: *get up, get over,
get by,* and *get after.*
   In the following sentences, multi-word verbs function as VT and are followed by
NP:DO:

a)   Keith **turned off** the lights.
b)   Christine **thought over** her answer to the problem.
c)   Kevin **puts up with** the noise from downstairs.
d)   Debbie is **counting on** a bull market.

Other multi-word verbs may function as VI:

e)   After working on the puzzle for two hours, Judy **gave up**.
f)   Katy **worked out** at the gym yesterday.

Some multi-word VTs are separable. The direct object may appear between the verb
and the particle:

g)   Keith **turned** the lights **off**.
h)   Christine **thought** the answer **over**.

When a separable multi-word VT has a pronoun object, the pronoun **must** occur between the V and the Prt:

i)   Kevin turned them off.
j)   * Kevin turned off them.
k)   Christine thought it over.
l)   *Christine thought over it.

Other multi-word verbs are **inseparable**:

  m) *Kevin **puts** the noise **up with**.
  n) *Kevin **puts up** the noise **with**.
  o) *Debbie is **counting** a bull market **on**.

When analyzing sentences, we are sometimes faced with the problem of deciding whether a structure is a V + Prt construction or a V + PP (prepositional phrase) construction:

  p) George **ran across** a good article in a magazine. (V + Prt = VT)
  q) George **ran** across the street. (VI + PP)
  r) Francine **turned down** the volume. (V + Prt = VT)
  s) Francine **turned** down the alley. (VI + PP)

Some clues for identifying V + Prt combinations.

  1) Your intuitions may help you. In a sentence like (p), "ran across" intuitively forms a constituent, and it seems fairly natural to pause briefly after "across." In sentence (q), "across the street" intuitively forms a constituent and it seems fairly natural to pause after "ran."

  2) If the verb and the following word can be separated by an intervening object, the structure is V + Prt. Remember, however, that not all V + Prt structures are separable.

  3) If you can attach a PP parallel to the existing structure, then it is a V + PP.

    t) George ran **across the street** and **into the store**. (across the street = PP)
    u) *George ran **across a good article** and **into a good story**. (across a good article is not a PP)

  4) PP structures can sometimes move around in a sentence. Moving a Prt and the NP following it often results in an ungrammatical structure.

    v) **Across the street** George ran. (across the street = PP)
    w) *Across a good article George ran.

  5) You can often insert a manner adverb between a V and a PP following it. However, you usually can't place a manner adverb between a V and a Prt.

    x) George ran quickly (angrily, hurriedly) across the street.
    y) *George ran quickly (*angrily, *hurriedly) across an article.

  6) V + Prt structures can often be replaced in a sentence by a single verb.

    z) Keith **turned off** the lights = Keith **extinguished** the lights.
    aa) Christine **thought over** her answers = Christine **pondered** her answers.
    bb) Kevin **puts up with** the noise = Kevin **tolerates** the noise.

Sentence Structure

NP: Subj	VP: Pred		

NP: Subj	Verb	Verb Complements	(Adverbs)

Things You Need to Know About
Verb Types

One of the most important things you need to remember is **not** to try to memorize lists of verbs that belong to each type, because verbs often have multiple meanings, and can belong to a number of different categories. Given that there are thousands of verbs, and an infinite number of possible sentences in English, do you really believe you can memorize which category each of the verbs in these sentences belongs to?

Instead, try to read carefully every sentence and analyze the verb type depending on the specific context in the sentence; i.e., by looking at the components to the right and to the left of the verb.

Examples	Verb Type	Verb Complements
(1) The President **left,** but the Vice-president remained.	(1) **VI**	(1) _____
(2) The president **left** the room.	(2) **VT**	(2) **DO** (the room)
(3) He **left** his wife and two children.	(3) **VT**	(3) **DO** (his wife and his two children)
(4) His decision **left** me disappointed.	(4) **Vc**	(4) **DO** (me) **OC (AdjP)** (disappointed)
(5) He **left** the doorman a note.	(5) **Vg**	(5) **DO** (a note) **IO** (the doorman)
(6) He **left** a note for the doorman.	(6) **Vg**	(6) **DO** (a note) **IO** (the doorman)
(1) The President left, but the Vice-president **remained.**	(1) **VI**	(1) _____
(2) She **remained** a president for two years.	(2) **VL**	(2) **PredN** (a president)

The reason "left" in *He left a note for the doorman* is a Vg (and not a Vc verb which also allows two NP complements) is that it represents a typical Vg situation with three separate entities: (1) "he" (the giver); (2) "a note" which is being given from him to the doorman; and (3) "the doorman" (the receiver). In addition, both the IO and the DO of the verb can become subjects in passive structures; e.g., ***The doorman*** *was given a note (by him),* and ***A note*** *was given to the doorman (by him).*

By contrast, "left" in *His decision left me disappointed* is a Vc verb because "his decision" did not "leave me," it "left me feeling disappointed," where "me" is the DO, and the AdjP "disappointed" completes the meaning of the DO "me," by describing or modifying it (in the same way as the PredAdj qualifies the Subject of the verb BE; e.g., *Because of his decision, I was disappointed*).

Things You Need to Know About

Verb Types

Examples	Verb Type	Verb Complements
(1) She **was** a doctor.	**(1) BE**	**(1) PredN** (a doctor) *She* and *a doctor* refer to the same person.
(2) She **became** a doctor.	**(2) VL**	**(2) PredN** (a doctor) *She* and *a doctor* refer to the same person.
(3) She **called** a doctor.	**(3) VT**	**(3) DO** (a doctor) *She* and *a doctor* refer to different people. She phoned a doctor/she called someone and asked for a doctor.
(4) She **called** him a doctor.	**(4) Vc** **Vg**	**(4) DO** (him), **OC (NP)** (a doctor) *Him* and *a doctor* refer to the same person. She addresses this person using the term *doctor.* **IO** (him), **DO** (a doctor) *She, him* and *a doctor* refer to three different people. She called a doctor for him.
(5) She **called** herself a doctor.	**(5) Vc** **Vg**	**(5) DO** (herself), **OC (NP)** (a doctor) *She, herself* and *a doctor* refer to the same person. She referred to herself using the term *doctor.* **IO** (herself), **DO** (a doctor) *She* and *herself* refer to the same person, but *a doctor* refers to a different person. She called a doctor for herself.
(6) She **called** him "Doctor."	**(6) Vc**	**(6) DO** (him), **OC (NP)** (doctor) *Doctor* without the IndefArt sounds like a term of address and, unlike (4), only allows the Vc interpretation.
(7) She **called** herself "Doctor."	**(7) Vc**	**(7) DO** (herself), **OC (NP)** (doctor) *Doctor* without the IndefArt sounds like a term of address and, like (6) but unlike (4), only allows the Vc interpretation.
(8) She **called** five minutes ago.	**(8) VI**	**(8)** _____

Verb Types Diagrams and Illustrations

Transitive Verbs

They   are building   **a new high-rise.**
Subj   VT   **DO**

Images courtesy of shutterstock.com

As mentioned above, transitive verbs can be made passive. Passivization may be illustrated in the following way:

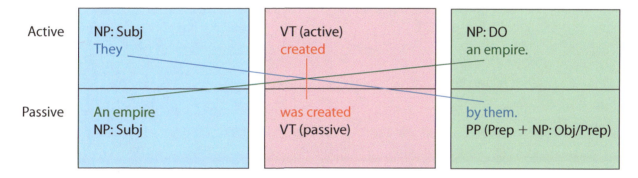

Active	NP: Subj They	VT (active) created	NP: DO an empire.
Passive	An empire NP: Subj	was created VT (passive)	by them. PP (Prep + NP: Obj/Prep)

Passives, questions, and sentences containing relative clauses, etc., are best analyzed if turned into active sentences, statements, and simple clauses, respectively. The transformations allow us to see if the verb has any complement, and which type it is.

Passive   The letter has not yet been written. _____

Active   They have not yet written the letter.
                     VT   **NP:DO**

Questions   What have you heard _____ about the accident?

Statements   You have heard what/something about the accident?
                     VT   **NP:DO**

RelCl   The gift that I bought is not expensive.

Simple   I bought a gift. The gift is not expensive.
          VT **NP:DO**

Vg Verbs

Vg verbs involve three separate entities. Imagine two baseball players, James (the pitcher) and Matt (the catcher), and one of them throwing a ball to the other.

James threw **Matt the ball.**
Subj Vg **IO** **DO**

James threw **the ball** to **Matt.**
Subj Vg **DO** **IO**

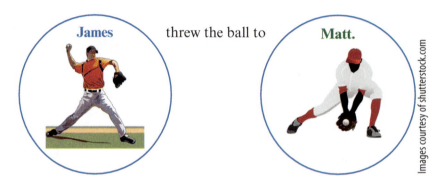

Linking Verbs

The NP:Subject and the predicate form (PredN or PredAdj) on both sides of the verb refer to the same entity. The PredN renames the subject, while the PredAdj modifies it.

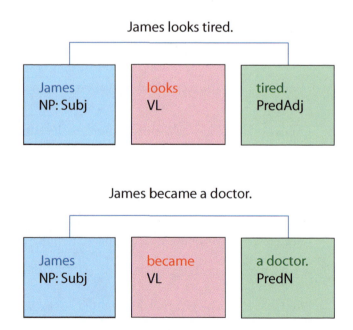

Intransitive Verbs

VI verbs do not normally require any complements.

Jane is running
Subj VI

James arrived.

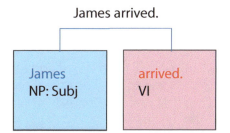

James	arrived.
NP: Subj	VI

The Verb BE

James   is   **in his office**
Subj   BE   **PredAdv**

The NP:Subject and the predicate form (PredN, PredAdj, or PredAdv) on both sides of the verb BE refer to the same entity. The PredN renames the subject (as in (a)), the PredAdj modifies it (as in (b)), and the PredAdv provides information about its place, time, accompaniment, etc. (as in (c)).

a)   James is a doctor.
b)   James is tired.
c)   James is here.
        James is on time.
        James is with his grandma.

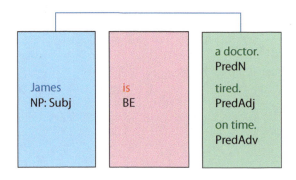

Vc Verbs

Here are several subtypes of Vc verbs:

a) like ***consider*** (expressing beliefs and opinions)
e.g., They <u>found</u> the experience unsettling.
b) like ***call*** (giving names, labels, etc.)
e.g., They <u>dubbed</u> him "the Killer".
c) like ***make*** (making people feel a certain way)
e.g., You <u>make</u> me happy.
d) like ***let*** (allowing or causing someone to do something)
e.g. <u>Let</u> me think about it.

The OC (NP, AdjP, or InfP) completes the meaning of the DO.

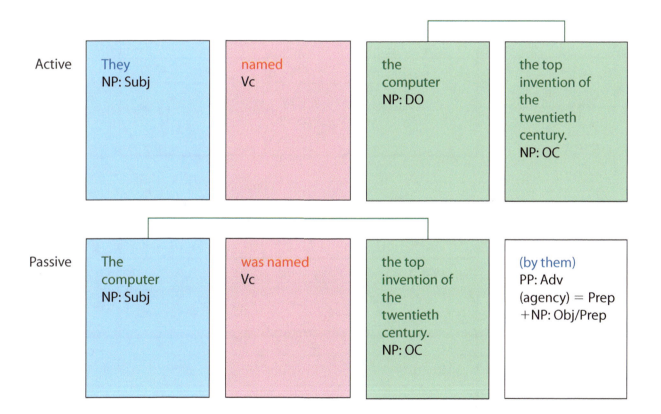

Verb Types and Verb Complements

	Verb Type	Verb Complements	(Adverbs)
NP:Subj	1. VI	-------	
	2. VL	PredN / PredAdj	
	3. VT	DO	
	4. Vg	IO DO DO (to/for) IO	
	5. Vc	DO OC → NP / AdjP / InfPh	
	6. BE	PredN / PredAdj / PredAdv	

	Verb Type	Verb Complements	(Adverbs)
They	1. arrived	-------	(at 5 o'clock)
	2. became	students / famous	(at SFU) 3 years ago)
	3. closed	the door	(quietly)
	4. bought	me flowers flowers for me	(yesterday)
	5. consider	him → a star / famous / to be a star	(in this city)
	6. are	students / famous / in class	(at SFU) (in this city) (this morning)

74

Exercises

A. Each group of sentences contains the same verb, but it may have a different meaning and therefore belong to a different verb type. Identify the type of the underlined verbs, choosing from the following: VI, VL, VT, Vg, Vc, or BE.

1. The child **looked** at the black cat. _____

   The child **looked** tired and unhappy. _____

   The child **looked** toward the ship. _____

2. GM **makes** cars and trucks. _____

   My mom **makes** me delicious cakes. _____

   This **makes** me happy. _____

3. He **went** outside. _____

   He **went** for a walk. _____

   He **went** to work. _____

   He **went** crazy, trying to solve this problem. _____

4. Melanie **wrote** for pleasure. _____

   Melanie **wrote** short stories for children. _____

   Melanie **wrote** her fans personal letters. _____

5. The old man **died** that afternoon in 1963. _____

   The villagers said the old man **died** a hero. _____

6. The meeting **will start** on time. _____

   I **will start** the meeting on time. _____

If you need more challenge, try out this exercise.

B. Identify each underlined verb as belonging to one of the six categories: VI, VL, VT, Vg, Vc, or BE. Then identify the verb complements, if any, by rewriting them and choosing one of the following labels: DO, IO, OC (specify if the OC is NP, AdjP, or InfP), PredN, PredAdj, PredAdv, or None.

Sentence	Verb Type	Verb Complement(s)
1. This LCD computer monitor sometimes **turns** blue, and then changes back to normal. [Why is My LCD . . . , yahoo.com]	1. _____	_____
2. No one **delivers** pizza as fast as Dominos. [from a Dominos commercial]	2. _____	_____
3. Many businesses **have offered** the city council support for its green roofs initiative.	3. _____	_____
4. The jeweler **made** them the most exquisite wedding rings from his new collection.	4. _____	_____
5. Students who **behave** inappropriately will be expelled from class.	5. _____	_____
6. Students who behave inappropriately **will be expelled** from class.	6. _____	_____
7. Do you really think you **are** qualified for this job?	7. _____	_____
8. You will have to **persevere** to be able to finish your degree on time.	8. _____	_____
9. My boss **deems** professional development days essential for our business.	9. _____	_____
10. The final agreement **was called** the Proclamation of Independence.	10. _____	_____
11. This is the worst joke I'**ve** ever **heard**.	11. _____	_____
12. The sun **disappeared** behind the majestic mountains.	12. _____	_____
13. We'll talk about how social media like Facebook and Twitter **impact** our daily lives. [adapted from "5 Ways Social Media . . . ," mashable.com]	13. _____	_____

Sentence	Verb Type	Verb Complement(s)
14. A note **was left** for the principal on the front door of the school.	14. _____	_____
15. The department created a supportive, non-critical environment where people **felt** comfortable and talked to each other openly about issues.	15. _____	_____
16. Dare to **think** the unthinkable, imagine the impossible, discuss the improbable. [from Philosophers' Café, sfu.ca]	16. _____	_____
17. Please send us your email address, so we can **keep** you electronically updated on the latest changes in the schedule.	17. _____	_____
18. Things **have** never **been** better.	18. _____	_____
19. Can science **be trusted?** [from Philosophers' Café, sfu.ca]	19. _____	_____
20. What does your intuition **tell** you? [from Philosophers' Café, sfu.ca]	20. _____	_____
21. We care about the environment because we want to **leave** our children a livable world.	21. _____	_____
22. Emily **found** the conditions in the hotel room appalling.	22. _____	_____
23. Somehow, things **went** wrong.	23. _____	_____
24. South Australia **was proclaimed** a colony in 1836. [adapted from governor.sa.gov.au]	24. _____	_____
25. The River Tiber, which runs through Rome, **has risen** to its highest level in four decades. [from "Floods Beset Italy . . . ," terradaily.com]	25. _____	_____

If you need more challenge, try out this exercise.

C. Identify each underlined word or group of words as one of the verb complements: DO, IO, OC, PredN, PredAdj, PredAdv, or indicate None.

1. They shouldn't be selling us **paper coffee cups which have plastic lids** since the plastic lids are non-recyclable.
[adapted from the radio clip "Problems with Coffee Cups," cbc.ca]

   1. _____

2. They shouldn't be selling **us** paper coffee cups which have plastic lids since the plastic lids are non-recyclable.

   2. _____

3. They shouldn't be selling us paper coffee cups with plastic lids since the plastic lids are **non-recyclable.**

   3. _____

4. We sent those packets **to Brazil** on Monday.

   4. _____

5. Children often take it for granted that parents will always be **by their side.**

   5. _____

6. The economic crisis made the need to cut costs **our top priority.**

   6. _____

7. The bad weather made the assignment they gave me **a dreaded experience.**

   7. _____

8. Could you please show **me** the way to New Westminster?

   8. _____

9. He quickly put himself together and knocked the thief **unconscious.**

   9. _____

10. This historian turned **novelist** and wrote a book about World War II.
[from "How a Historian . . . ," hnn.us]

   10. _____

Answers to Exercises

A.
1. The child **looked** at the black cat.
The child **looked** tired and unhappy.
The child **looked** toward the ship.

1. VI
VL
VI

2. GM **makes** cars and trucks.
My mom **makes** me delicious cakes.

This **makes** me happy.

2. VT
Vg (My mom makes delicious cakes for me)
Vc

3. He **went** outside.
He **went** for a walk.

He **went** to work.
He **went** crazy, trying to solve this problem.

3. VI
VI (idiomatic; alternatively, "go for" VT-2 wds, similar to "take")
VI
VL

4. Melanie **wrote** for pleasure.

Melanie **wrote** short stories for children.
Melanie **wrote** her fans personal letters.

4. VI (some sources claim it is a VT, with an implied DO; e.g., books)
VT or **Vg**
Vg

5. The old man **died** that afternoon in 1963.
The villagers said the old man **died** a hero.

5. VI
VL

6. The meeting **will start** on time.
I **will start** the meeting on time.

6. VI
VT

B.

Sentence	Verb Type	Verb Complement(s)
1. turns	VL	■ blue: PredAdj
2. delivers	VT	■ pizza: DO
3. have offered	Vg	■ the city council: IO ■ support for its green roofs initiative: DO
4. made	Vg	■ them: IO ■ the most exquisite wedding rings from his new collection: DO
5. behave	VI	_____

Sentence	Verb Type	Verb Complement(s)
6. will be expelled	VT	_____ *[in the active, "The school/they will expel* **students** *(**DO**) . . .]*
7. are	BE	■ qualified for this job: PredAdj
8. persevere	VI	_____
9. deems	Vc	■ professional development days: DO ■ essential for our business: OC:AdjP
10. was called	Vc	■ the Proclamation of Independence : OC:NP
11. 've heard	VT	■ the worst joke: DO *[I've heard the worst joke (DO)]*
12. disappeared	VI	_____
13. impacts	VT	■ our daily lives: DO
14. was left	Vg	■ for the principal: IO (active "Someone left a note for the principal")
15. felt	VL	■ comfortable: PredAdj
16. think	VT	■ the unthinkable: DO
17. keep	Vc	■ you: DO ■ electronically updated on the latest changes in the schedule: OC:AdjP
18. have been	BE	■ better: PredAdj
19. be trusted	VT	_____ *[active :"Can we/one/people trust science (DO)?"]*
20. tell	Vg	■ you: IO ■ what: DO
21. leave	Vg	■ our children: IO ■ a livable world: DO
22. found	Vc	■ the conditions in the hotel room: DO ■ appalling: OC:AdjP
23. went	VL	■ wrong: PredAdj

Sentence	Verb Type	Verb Complement(s)
24. <u>**was proclaimed**</u>	**Vc**	■ a colony: OC:NP *[in the active: "They proclaimed South Australia (DO) a colony . . ."]*
25. <u>**has risen**</u>	**VI**	_____

C.
1. **DO**
2. **IO**
3. **PredAdj**
4. **None**   **(Adv; not a verb complement)**
5. **PredAdv**
6. **OC**
7. **OC**
8. **IO**
9. **OC**
10. **PredN**

Status of Verbs: Tense, Aspect, and Voice

CHAPTER 5

1) Verbs in English are traditionally said to have five forms or "parts."

Parts of the verb	Remarks	Examples
base form	can occur after *to*	work, eat, write
third person singular	can occur after *she, he,* or *it*	works, eats, writes
present participle	always ends in *-ing*	working, eating, writing
past tense	occurs without an auxiliary	worked, ate, wrote
past participle	can occur after *have*	worked, eaten, written

2) The main verb constituent (MV) is the unit containing the verb and any auxiliaries.

3) English is usually said to have two "morphological tenses": present and past. The tense can generally be determined by looking at the first word in the MV.

Tense	Examples
present tense	**works**, **is** eating, **have** been writing
past tense	**worked**, **had** eaten, **had** been writing

It's very important to understand that *tense* and *time* are not the same thing. *Tense* is a grammatical notion. Different languages may use tenses in very different ways. *Time,* on the other hand, refers to a concept that is common to all human experience. It is understood in terms of past, present, and future. The relationship between tense and time is not straightforward. For instance, in English we have no morphological future tense. But that certainly doesn't mean that we can't talk about future time. Here are some examples:

I'm leaving tomorrow. (present tense, future time)
I **will leave** tomorrow. (modal "will," future time)
Yesterday, he told me that he **wasn't leaving** till next week. (past tense, future time)

Here is another illustration of the complexity of the tense and time relationship:

I have already finished my homework. (present tense, past time)

Quick Quiz		
What, **in your opinion**, are the past tense and past participle forms of the following verbs? Are there any that you are unsure of? Why?		
Verb	Past tense	Past Participle
Shrink		
Bid		
Stink		
Hang		
Sneak		
Lie		
Lay		
Swing		
Forsake		
Thrive		
Shoe		

4) Some MVs contain a modal.

>   **Examples:** will work, should have worked, might have been working

Do modals have tense?

You should be aware that some textbooks (including Morenberg 2010:54) consider modals to have present forms (e.g., can, will, shall) and past forms (could, would, should). This seems to make sense in pairs such as the following:

>   This year she can run a mile in five minutes. (present ability)
>   Last year she could run a mile in six minutes. (past ability)

Although we will follow Morenberg's approach, analyzing modals strictly in this way doesn't buy us much in terms of helping us understand them. Modals convey a wide range of meanings, many of which have little to do with present versus past time. The difference between *can* and *could,* for instance, is different in many respects from the distinction between walk and walked. How would you characterize the distinctions that are made in these sentences?

Can you open the window, please?
Could you open the window, please?
Would you open the window, please?

We'll consider some ways of describing the meanings of modals later.

5) The two kinds of aspect are progressive (also called continuous) and perfective or perfect.

Progressive aspect can be recognized by the presence of the following:

be + present participle (-ing form) of the verb
be + . . . + ing

She **is** driv**ing.** (present tense + progressive aspect)
She **was** driv**ing.** (past tense + progressive aspect)
She may **be** driv**ing.** (present modal + progressive aspect)

Perfective aspect can be recognized by the presence of the following:

have + past participle of the verb
have + . . . + ed/en/etc.

She **has** driv**en.** (present tense + perfective aspect)
She **had** driv**en.** (past tense + perfective aspect)
She may **have** driv**en.** (present modal + perfective aspect)

6) When both kinds of aspect are evident, the auxiliary indicating the perfective *(have)* precedes.

She **has** been driving. (present tense + perfective aspect + progressive aspect)
She **had** been driving. (past tense + perfective aspect + progressive aspect)
She may **have** been driving. (present modal + perfective aspect + progressive aspect)

7) Voice may be active or passive.

Active voice

In active sentences, the subject is often the "doer of an action."

The legislature passed a law.

Passive voice

In passive sentences, the subject often undergoes an action. The doer of the action is indicated in a prepositional phrase beginning with "by," or it may be omitted.

A law was passed by the legislature.
A law was passed.

Passive voice may be recognized by the presence of the following:

be + past participle of the verb
be + . . . + ed/en/etc.

She **is** driv**en** (by George). (simple present tense, passive voice)
A law **was** pass**ed** (by the legislature). (simple past tense, passive voice)

8) When the passive voice is used together with one or both kinds of aspect, the auxiliary indicating the passive (be) comes last before the verb.

She is **being** driven. (present tense + progressive aspect + passive voice)
She has been **being** driven. (present tense + perfective aspect + prog. aspect + passive voice)

9) Here is a summary table, showing examples of the possible combinations of tense, aspect and voice.

Tense	Aspect	Active Voice	Passive Voice
simple present	—	she works	she is driven
present	progressive	she is working	she is being driven
present	perfect	she has worked	she has been driven
present	perfect progressive	she has been working	she has been being driven
simple past	—	she worked	she was driven
past	progressive	she was working	she was being driven
past	perfect	she had worked	she had been driven
past	perfect progressive	she had been working	she had been being driven

Notice that the present perfect progressive passive and the past perfect progressive passive are quite cumbersome structures, and they are rarely used in spoken or written English. However, they are grammatical, and it is not difficult to imagine contexts in which these forms might be appropriate.

Things You Need to Know About

Tense, Aspect, and Voice

There are only two morphologically-marked **tenses** in English:

- **present** *(he stays),* marked with the inflection "-s" in the third person singular, and
- **past** *(he stayed),* marked with the inflection "-ed."

English uses other means to express future; e.g.,

- modals like *will,*
- catenatives like *be going to,*
- adverbs like *tomorrow.*

The main verb is the verb along with its auxiliary elements (e.g., *may, shall, have, is)*; i.e., the forms that show its:

- tense,
- modality,
- voice, and
- aspect.

The following diagram illustrates some of the elements that comprise the main verb in English. Note that they are not necessarily used at the same time, and some are mutually exclusive; e.g., the past tense marker "-ed" and the present-tense marker "-s."

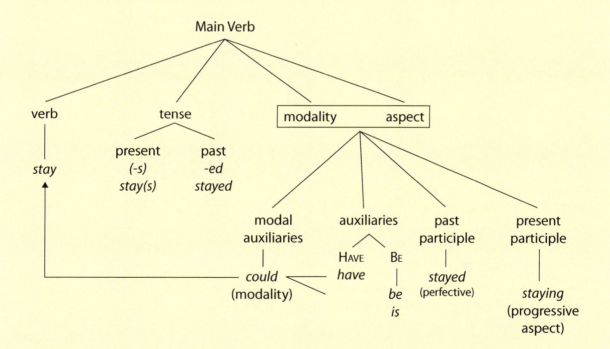

Tense is marked **only once** in the main verb, and **always on the first element** of the verb; e.g., if the first element is Aux "BE," it gets the tense marker (e.g., he **was** building a house); if the first element is a modal, it gets the tense (e.g., he **could** have built a house).

Things You Need to Know About

Tense, Aspect, and Voice

- All forms that show tense are called **finite,**
- while all forms that do **not** show tense, and whose form remains unchanged regardless of the time of the event and who is involved in it, are called **non-finite.**

For example, the present participle *writing* does **not** show tense or change its form, regardless of the time of the event or the number and gender of the doers of the activity.

Tense and Time	Example	Gender and Number of the Subject
Present tense and time	He is **writing** a novel.	masculine, singular
	They are **writing** a novel.	plural
Past tense and time	She was **writing** a novel at that time.	feminine, singular
Present tense, future time	She will be **writing** a novel at that time.	feminine, singular

Aspect indicates that the action of a verb is either completed (perfect aspect) or continuing (progressive aspect).

Perfect aspect indicates that the action of a verb is completed. - It is shown by the auxiliary HAVE and the past participle (e.g., *She **has seen** him before*). - The auxiliary HAVE exhibits tense: 　- present perfect (***has*** seen); or 　- past perfect (***had*** seen). - Despite the terms (e.g., present perfect), **both** are related to completed actions.	**Progressive aspect** indicates that the action is continuing. - It is shown by the auxiliary BE and the present participle (e.g., *She **is dancing***). - The auxiliary BE exhibits **tense:** 　- present progressive (***is*** dancing), or 　- past progressive (***was*** dancing). - The terms present and past refer only to the form of BE.

It is possible for **the perfect and progressive aspect to occur together**; e.g., "he has been studying at SFU for three years now," where:

- **the perfect aspect** indicates that a three-year period of studying has been completed, while
- **the progressive aspect** indicates that the activity is still in progress.

Things You Need to Know About

Tense, Aspect, and Voice

The category of **voice** is related to the semantic category of agent or doer of the action, and patient or experiencer of the action.

In **active** constructions, the agent (or doer of the action) and the subject coincide; e.g.,
 	
Jane S. Parker wrote the novel in 1939.
 	
 ■ "Jane S. Parker" is both the grammatical subject and the person who wrote the novel.
	In **passive** constructions, the patient (or experiencer, or entity that has been acted upon) and the subject coincide; e.g.,
	
	The novel was written in 1939 (by Jane S. Parker).
	
	 ■ "The novel" is only the grammatical subject; novels don't write themselves.
	
	 ■ It is still Jane S. Parker who wrote the novel in 1939; therefore "Jane S. Parker" in the prepositional phrase with "by" is called the logical subject.
	
	 ■ The easiest way **to recognize a passive structure** such as *The letter was sent over the email* is:
	
	  ■ to ask yourself "Who did the action?" and
	  ■ if you can't tell, or if you see the answer in the by-phrase, the structure is passive.
	
	 ■ The easiest way **to analyze the verb in a passive structure** such as *The letter was sent over the email* is:
	
	  ■ to turn the passive sentence back into active; e.g., *Someone sent the letter over the email,* and
	  ■ see what kind of verb complements the verb has, if any; e.g., "the letter" is the DO of the VT "sent."

Exercises

A. The word "smoking" is used in all of these sentences. In which of them is it the present participle form of the verb? Can you tell what it is if it is not a participle?

Sentence		Answer	
a)	*This is a **smoking** area.*	**a)**	_____
b)	*She is **smoking** hot.*	**b)**	_____
c)	*She is **smoking**.*	**c)**	_____
d)	*Is **smoking** really dangerous?*	**d)**	_____
e)	*We were just talking about **smoking**.*	**e)**	_____
f)	*We were **smoking** on the porch when the phone rang.*	**f)**	_____
g)	*She called **smoking** suicide.*	**g)**	_____
h)	*She hasn't been **smoking** for over five years now.*	**h)**	_____

B. Study the sentences below, and underline the parts of the main verbs that show tense. Then decide if the forms listed in the table can exhibit tense or not. Next to your answer "yes" or "no," you may indicate the number of the example that supports your decision.

1. Did he stay here last year?

2. I'm thinking about this possibility.

3. When I saw this question on the exam, I couldn't answer it.

4. She loves risk, adventure, and high-adrenaline experiences.

5. I got fired last week from the only job I've ever liked.

6. I wasn't able to get to this until Friday afternoon.

Can these forms exhibit tense?	Yes	No
a) single verbs without auxiliaries		
b) the base forms of verbs following auxiliaries		
c) the auxiliary "be"		
d) the auxiliary "have"		
e) the auxiliary "do"		
f) the auxiliary "get"		
g) modals		
h) catenatives		

C. Put the verb "study" in the requested tense-aspect form.

1. Tense + Verb   **1.** _____

2. Tense + Modal + Verb   **2.** _____

3. Tense + Perfect + Verb   **3.** _____

4. Tense + Progressive + Verb   **4.** _____

5. Tense + Modal + Perfect + Verb   **5.** _____

6. Tense + Modal + Progressive + Verb   **6.** _____

7. Tense + Perfect + Progressive + Verb   **7.** _____

8. Tense + Modal + Perfect + Progressive + Verb **8.** _____

Answers to Exercises

A.
 a) **Noun functioning as an Adjective**
 b) **Qualifier** (of "hot"—"informal")
 c) **Present Participle (VI)** (Present Progressive Aspect)
 d) **Noun,** more specifically **Gerund (VI) functioning as a Subject**
 e) **Noun,** more specifically **Gerund (VI) functioning as the Obj/Prep** "about"
 f) **Present Participle(VI)** (Past Progressive Aspect)
 g) **Noun,** more specifically **Gerund (VI) functioning as a DO** of Vc "called"
 h) **Present Participle (VI)** (Present Perfect Progressive Aspect—Neg)

B.
 1. <u>**Did**</u> he stay here last year?
 2. I'<u>**m**</u> thinking about this possibility.
 3. When I <u>**saw**</u> this question on the exam, I <u>**couldn't**</u> answer it.
 4. She <u>**loves**</u> risk, adventure, and high-adrenaline experiences.
 5. I <u>**got**</u> fired last week from the only job I'<u>**ve**</u> ever liked.
 6. I <u>**wasn't able to**</u> get to this until Friday afternoon.

Can these forms exhibit tense?	Yes	No
a) single verbs without auxiliaries	✔ sentence 3 (saw), sentence 4 (loves)	
b) the base forms of verbs following auxiliaries		✔ sentence 1 (stay), sentence 3 (answer), sentence 6 (get)
c) the auxiliary "be"	✔ sentence 2 ('m)	
d) the auxiliary "have"	✔ sentence 5 ('ve)	
e) the auxiliary "do"	✔ sentence 1 (did)	
f) the auxiliary "get"	✔ sentence 5 (got)	
g) modals	✔ sentence 3 (could)	
h) catenatives	✔ sentence 6 (was able to)	

C.
 1. studies
 2. should study
 3. has studied
 4. is studying
 5. should have studied
 6. should be studying
 7. has been studying
 8. should have been studying

Using English Tense and Aspect

In this section, we will summarize a few of the common uses of various tense/aspect combinations. You should be aware that we have omitted many possibilities. In each case, consider the ways in which we might represent tense and aspect on the graph.

1. Simple Present

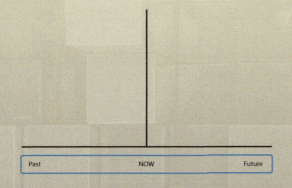

| Past | NOW | Future |

a) *Information presented as a fact (even if it isn't true!)*

> The sky is blue.
> Ron lives in Toronto.
> Grass is usually orange.

b) *Repeated or habitual actions*

> I get up at seven every day.
> Judy always drinks coffee for breakfast.

c) *Senses, perceptions, and desires*

I smell garlic.
Susie hears music playing.
I want mustard in my sandwich.

d) *Future events (especially scheduled events)*

The plane leaves tomorrow at seven.
Next week, Alan gets new office furniture.

e) *Narrative descriptions*

First, she gets on the plane. Then she meets a stranger. (describing a story, film, etc.)

2. Present Progressive

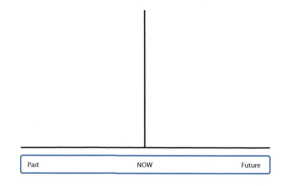

a) *Actions occurring at the present moment*

Don't bother me! I'm talking on the phone. (cf. I talk on the phone all the time.)
She's sitting in the back of the room.

b) *Actions occurring intermittently over a period that encompasses the present time. Such actions may or may not be in progress at the actual moment of speaking.*

Frederick is writing a novel.
They're shooting a new film on the island.

c) *Future events*

They're leaving first thing in the morning.
Carol is moving next month.

d)   *Narratives about past actions*

> So yesterday I'm walking down Main Street, and I see this guy with a parrot. He's carrying the parrot on his shoulder.

3. Simple Past

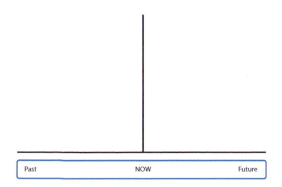

Actions or states at a specified or unspecified point in the past

> Nancy ate breakfast.
> Nancy ate breakfast at 6:30.
> Nancy ate breakfast two hours ago.
> Richard was tired.

4. Past Progressive

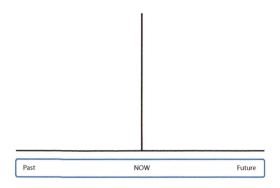

a)   *Actions or states in progress at a specified time or period of time in the past*

Jim was sleeping when the earthquake occurred.
What were you doing at 10:00 p.m. on the night of the murder?

b)   *Statements about the past in which the duration of an activity is emphasized.*

I was driving for over ten hours!
Joe was eating out of a can for six weeks!

5. Present Perfect

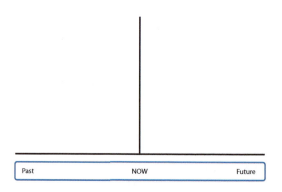

a)   *Events and states that began in the past, have continued to the present time, and have some likelihood of continuing into the future.*

Ann has lived in Vancouver for many years. (cf. Ann lived in Vancouver for many years.)

b)   *Events occurring within **a time frame** that began in the past and that continues up to the moment of speaking. Such events have at least a possibility of recurring in or persisting into the future.*

Alice Munro has written many short stories. (cf. ? Shakespeare has written many plays.)
I've graded 72 essays so far this week.
He has lived in Toronto, Calgary, and Winnipeg, though he now lives in Ottawa. (cf. He lived in Toronto, Calgary, and Winnipeg, but now he's dead.) (cf. *He has lived in Toronto, Calgary, and Winnipeg, but now he's dead.)
He has never eaten escargots. (He hasn't eaten escargots *so far* in his life, but he might do so at some time in the future.)
Have you ever traveled in a balloon? (The time frame of interest extends from the beginning of the addressee's life to the moment of speaking.)

c) *Events from the recent past that have some relevance to the present.*

> The doughnuts have just arrived.
> Frank has finished his paperwork.

The present perfect is not used for a single event when a point in time is specified.

> Caroline studied last night. (cf. * Caroline has studied last night).
> The letter arrived at six. (cf. * The letter has arrived at six.)

6. Past Perfect

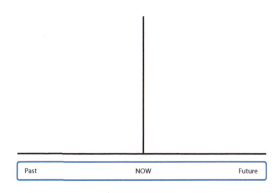

a) *Events occurring before and lasting until a particular time in the past*

> By June of last year, Rose had saved $500.

b) *Events occurring within a time frame that began and ended in the past.*

> By June of last year, Rose had lived in Toronto, Calgary, and Winnipeg.
> By June of last year, Rose had never eaten escargots.

c) *Events occurring immediately before a particular time in the past*

> Julia Child had finished cooking when Jacques Pepin arrived.

7. Present Perfect Progressive and Past Perfect Progressive

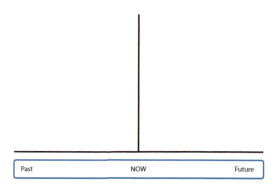

These can often substitute for the present perfect and past perfect. They emphasize that the event occurred over time.

I have been working for hours. (cf. I've worked for hours.)
Julia had been cooking for hours when Jacques arrived.

Things You Need to Know About

Using English Tense and Aspect

The terms tense and time are not identical. **Tense** is a grammatical category and "determines the physical form of the verb" (Morenberg 2010:51), while **time** refers to real time. Time in the western world is often visualized as a line with a single dot marking the present moment or now. The past is before now, schematically presented to the left of now, while the future is after now, schematically presented to the right of now.

Now

← Past   Present   Future →

The following examples illustrate how the same grammatical **tense**—present, can refer to present, past, and future **time**.

Examples	Tense	Time
(1) *He is working on his paper.*	**(1a)(1b)** | present | progressive tense	**(1a)** the event occurs at **the moment of speaking** **(1b)** he may not be working on the paper right this minute, but it's his main project this month; the event occurs during a period of time that includes **the moment of speaking** ⇒ | now | or | extended now |
(2) *He works at the department store.*	**(2)** | present | simple tense	**(2a)** this is his **current** job, and he is working **now** **(2b)** this is his **current** job, but he may **not** be working **right now** ⇒ | now | or | not right now |
(3) *The train leaves / is leaving at 8:00 p.m.*	**(3)** | present | simple/ progressive tense	**(3)** with events following a plan or schedule | future | time
(4) *And I go into the cafe last night, and I see her sitting alone at the corner table, drinking, and I ask her . . .*	**(4)** **present** simple tense	**(4)** for more immediate or vivid effect in story-telling, etc. with events that happened in the past ⇒ | past | time

Exercises

Analyze the following sentences according to these instructions:

   a. Identify the main verb (MV) by rewriting it and labeling it as one of these categories: VI, VL, VT, Vc, Vg, and BE in the MV column;

   b. Identify the MV's tense and aspect in the Tense and Aspect columns respectively;

   c. Identify the parts of multi-word MVs using the following labels:

Modal	Aux-DO	BASE (the verb after Aux)
Aux-BE	Aux-HAVE	NEG
PastPart (past participle)		V (for one-word verbs)
PresPart (present participle)		Caten (catenative/semi-modal)

   d. Identify the DO, IO, OC (and its type: NP, AdjP, InfP), PredN, PredAdj, and PredAdv in the Verb complements column.

Examples:

   1. These two actors play the game perfectly in Hollywood.

   2. He may be studying now.

Answer:

#	Main Verb and Type	Tense	Aspect	Verb Parts	Verb Complements
1	play: VT	present	——	V 'play'	the game: DO
2	may be studying: VI	present	progressive	Modal+Aux-BE +PresPart	—————

   1. It must have been snowing for a few hours already.
   2. They'll find you a replacement quickly.
   3. Is mom making us ice-cream?
   4. I'm not going to look this word up in a dictionary.
   5. They are throwing him a surprise birthday party.
   6. I'll order him a taxi for five o'clock.
   7. The building could have been sinking for years.
   8. She's not going to be able to pick him up from the airport.

#	Main Verb and Type	Tense	Aspect	Verb Parts	Verb Complements
1					
2					
3					
4					
5					
6					
7					
8					

Answers to the Exercises

#	Main Verb and Type	Tense	Aspect	Verb Parts	Verb Complements
1	must have been snowing: VI	present	perfect progressive	Modal+Aux-Have +Aux-BE+PresPart	_____
2	'll find: Vg	present	_____	Modal+Base 'find'	■ you: IO (=for you) ■ a replacement: DO
3	is making: Vg	present	progressive	Aux-BE+PresPart	■ us: IO (=for us) ■ ice-cream: DO
4	'm not going to look up: VT	present	_____	Caten BE GOING TO[1] +NEG+Base (2 wds) 'look up'	■ this word: DO
5	are throwing: Vg	present	progressive	Aux-BE+PresPart	■ him: IO (=for him); ■ a surprise birthday party: DO
6	'll order: Vg	present	_____	Modal+Base 'order'	■ him: IO (=for him); ■ a taxi: DO
7	could have been sinking: VI	past	perfect progressive	Modal+Aux-Have +Aux-BE+PresPart	_____
8	's not going to be able to pick up: VT	present	_____	Caten BE GOING TO[1] +NEG + Caten BE ABLE TO + Base (2 wds) 'pick up'	■ him: DO

[1]Some grammarians treat "**to be going to**" and "**be able to**" as catenatives. However, catenatives generally require DO-support for negation and interrogation, while these two structures do not. In addition, some catenatives can be converted to "-ing" forms, as in *They're always having to/wanting to/needing to . . .* , while "be going to" has no form without "-ing."

Mood and Modals

Mood

1) Indicative: statements

> Flynn played Robin Hood in the movie.

2) Interrogative: questions

> Are you busy?
> What time is it?
> You're busy?

3) Imperative: instructions and commands

> Get up!
> Have some pie.

4) Conditional: expressions of possibility, probability, necessity, desire, doubt, obligation, and other related notions.

> You shouldn't buy a leaky condo.
> He may be right.

Uses of Modals

Modals convey many kinds of meanings, some of which differ from each other in quite subtle ways. As a result, modals are sometimes difficult to talk about and difficult for ESL learners to acquire. To make matters even more complicated, sentences with modals are often ambiguous—they may sometimes be interpreted in more than one way, depending on the context. Three particular kinds of meanings are described here.

1) **Epistemic** meaning has to do with the speaker's (or writer's) belief about some possible or necessary state of affairs.

Sentence	*Interpretation*
Tomorrow it **might** rain.	*The speaker believes that rain is possible (though he or she does not know for sure).*
Joe's coat is on the rack. He **must** be in his office.	*The speaker can infer that Joe is in his office because his coat is here.*
I can't find my keys. I **may** have left them in the car.	*The speaker judges that it is possible that the keys were left in the car.*

2) **Deontic** meaning has to do with the speaker's intention to influence someone or something. When a modal has this type of meaning it typically indicates advice, permission, or an instruction by the speaker to do something.

Sentence	*Interpretation*
Anna **can** have another cookie if she likes.	*The speaker gives Anna permission to have another cookie.*
I'm not interested in talking to you. You **must** leave right now!	*The speaker orders you to leave now.*
Elaine **should** get more rest. She looks tired.	*The speaker recommends that Elaine get more rest.*

3) **Dynamic** meanings typically indicate ability or willingness. Rather than reflecting the speaker's belief or desire to influence, modals with this kind of meaning generally refer to facts outside the speaker's judgment or control.

Sentence	*Interpretation*
Frank can play hockey very well.	*He has the ability to play hockey well.*
George won't help me fix the washer.	*George refuses to assist me.*

P **Prescriptive Note:** It is sometimes claimed that "can" is not to be used to indicate permission (i.e., in the deontic sense). In fact, "can" is almost universally used with that meaning in WCE and other varieties of English spoken in North America.

Quick Quiz

State whether the modals in these sentences have epistemic (E), deontic (DE), or dynamic (DY) meanings. Which ones are ambiguous?

1) There's a fly in the kitchen. You shouldn't have left the window open.   _____

2) If you have difficulty, Wilbur will assist you.   _____

3) You may kiss the bride.   _____

4) Her eyes are red. She must have been crying.   _____

5) I can open that door for you.   _____

6) There might be some chocolate cake in the fridge.   _____

7) There must be a better way to make a living than telemarketing.   _____

8) When I was younger, I could run ten kilometres with no difficulty.   _____

9) You can't be serious!   _____

10) May I have another chocolate, darling?   _____

Things You Need to Know About

Mood and Modals

Mood and **Modality** have to do with the purpose of the sentence.

Mood	Examples
(1) Indicative mood: a sentence providing information or making a statement: ■ has the following word order: Subject-Verb-Verb Complements, if any	**(1)** It was snowing on Burnaby Mountain yesterday. They just had a baby.
(2) Interrogative mood: a sentence asking a question; it is characterized by: ■ a different word order (called subject-verb inversion): Verb-Subject or Aux-Subject-Verb ■ rising intonation (e.g., on "Yes-No" questions) ■ use of interrogative pronouns, pro-adverbs, and pro-determiners in "Wh-" questions (e.g., who, when, whose, etc.)	**(2)** Was it snowing on Burnaby Mountain yesterday? Have you heard of this dinosaur before? Where are they?
(3) Imperative mood: a sentence giving a command: ■ the only type of sentence in English which normally does not have a subject ■ the implied addressee is usually "you" (singular or plural) ■ occasionally, the subject is stated explicitly ■ many grammarians call imperatives tenseless	**(3)** Go get my book! Hey, you, give me this!
(4) Conditional mood: a sentence indicating possibility or eventuality: ■ conditional sentences with "if" indicating that if a condition is met, a result will follow ■ sentences with modal verbs[1] (e.g., can, must, might, should, etc.)	**(4)** If it snows again on Burnaby Mountain, I'll have to put the snow tires back on my car. It may snow again this week on Burnaby Mountain.

[1]Students often ask about questions containing modal verbs; e.g., *Could you give me the book?* Such sentences are interrogative.

Modal verbs can be divided into categories depending on their form and meaning. Based on the morphological tense they exhibit, they have past and present forms, but you need to keep in mind that these forms rarely indicate past and present time respectively (see Ch. 5). For example, the modal verb "could" in a sentence like "Could you pass me the salt, please?" is past in form, but the verb "could pass" clearly refers to future time. Therefore, the following table refers only to the physical form of modal verbs.

Modal Verbs	
Present Form	Past Form
can shall will may must*	could should would might

*(only present form); e.g., *he must go*

A number of verbs called "catenative verbs" (or "catenatives," or "semi-modals") also function as auxiliaries and have similar meanings to those of modals. As you can see in the table below, they consist of two or three words, so we will be labeling them that way; e.g., "want to" Caten (2 wds).

Catenative (Semi-modal) Verbs	
Two-Word Catenatives	Three-Word Catenatives[2]
dare to happen to have to need to ought to seem to used to want to	be able to be going to be about to

[2]See note 1 in the answers to the exercises in Chapter 6.

Modals and **catenatives** always occur first in the main verb and exhibit tense. The verb following the modal is always in its **nonfinite** form; e.g.:

will come
will—present modal
come—non-finite verb

Modals and catenatives have three types of meaning: epistemic, deontic, and dynamic.

Meanings of Modals and Some Catenatives	Examples
(1) **Epistemic:** has to do with the speaker's belief about some possible or necessary state of affairs:	
a) future possibility (prediction); various degrees of certainty about this possibility	**Higher Degree of Certainty** **a)** It **will** be/**is going to** be sunny tomorrow. It **should/must/has to** be sunny tomorrow. It **may/might/could** be sunny tomorrow. **Lower Degree of Certainty** He **won't** tell his family about the accident. (prediction about the future)
b) **present possibility** (logical deduction or inference about present state of affairs)	**b)** His keys are on the table. He **must** be home./He **has to** be home.
c) **past possibility** (logical deduction or inference about past state of affairs) with perfective modals	**c)** We emailed her a reminder about the meeting, but she **may not have** checked her email.
(2) **Deontic:** has to do with the speaker's intention to influence someone or something, by giving:	
a) **advice** or **recommendation**	**a)** You look stressed out. You **need to** take it easy.
b) **permission**	**b)** You **may** start filling in the answer sheet now.
c) **instruction for the addressee to do something**	**c)** We're late! You **have to** run.
(3) **Dynamic:** generally refers to facts outside the speaker's judgment or control; usually has to do with:	
a) **ability** or **skill**	**a)** When she was five, she **could** lift this table by herself. **Can** you play the accordion with one hand?
b) someone other than the speaker's **willingness** or **desire** to do something	**b)** He **won't** tell his family about the accident. (=he doesn't want to tell his family)

Exercises

A. Underline the complete MV in each sentence. Indicate the verb type (VI, VT, Vc, etc.), and then list the mood, modals, tense, aspect, and voice. If any of these is missing, write "none."

1. George reported the accident.

       Mood: Modals: Tense: Aspect: Voice:

2. Several of the trees in our yard were severely damaged by the storm.

       Mood: Modals: Tense: Aspect: Voice:

3. Why have the doors been left open again?

       Mood: Modals: Tense: Aspect: Voice:

4. Jim may have forgotten to give you a call.

       Mood: Modals: Tense: Aspect: Voice:

5. Has the car been running well?

       Mood: Modals: Tense: Aspect: Voice:

6. Didn't you put the cat outside last night?

       Mood: Modals: Tense: Aspect: Voice:

7. That shirt is quite becoming on you.

       Mood: Modals: Tense: Aspect: Voice:

8. On Tuesday, I will have been living here for seven years.

       Mood: Modals: Tense: Aspect: Voice:

9. I'm always being paged!

       Mood: Modals: Tense: Aspect: Voice:

10. Have you been helped?

       Mood: Modals: Tense: Aspect: Voice:

11. The dissidents are gradually being eliminated.

Mood: Modals: Tense: Aspect: Voice:

12. Give me one reason to stay here.

Mood: Modals: Tense: Aspect: Voice:

13. Carol doesn't like working overtime.

Mood: Modals: Tense: Aspect: Voice:

14. She's only been home a week.

Mood: Modals: Tense: Aspect: Voice:

15. Jill has just gotten over a cold.

Mood: Modals: Tense: Aspect: Voice:

16. Jack hates cooking dinner.

Mood: Modals: Tense: Aspect: Voice:

17. Pass me the salt, please.

Mood: Modals: Tense: Aspect: Voice:

18. Our customers are always treated with courtesy.

Mood: Modals: Tense: Aspect: Voice:

19. The fridge hadn't been cleaned in over a month.

Mood: Modals: Tense: Aspect: Voice:

20. She must have been worrying all evening.

Mood: Modals: Tense: Aspect: Voice:

B. Which of these words best describes the meaning of the modal or catenative in each sentence?

ability   advice   instruction
necessity   permission   possibility
promise   willingness

Based on your choice, determine if the meaning of each modal or catenative is epistemic (E), deontic (DE), or dynamic (DY):

1. The packet **may** be coming in the mail this week.   _____ _____

2. This nonsense **has to** stop right now.   _____ _____

3. If he **can't** do it, I don't know who **can.**   _____ _____

4. You **may** come in.   _____ _____

5. O.k., fine, I **will** do it.   _____ _____

6. I **could have** come to the party if I knew the address.   _____ _____

7. You **need to** ask before taking your dad's car.   _____ _____

8. No one **was able to** tell what happened.   _____ _____

9. You **must** use a different approach to solve the problem.   _____ _____

10. You **shouldn't have** taken your dad's car without permission.   _____ _____

11. He **is not going to** give you a raise, no matter what you do.   _____ _____

12. I hear voices inside. There **must** be someone in the house.   _____ _____

C. Which sentence in each pair expresses a higher degree of certainty about a possibility in the past, present or future? Circle it.

Then, based on your choice, write a short sentence creating an appropriate context for each of the sentences.

1. **a)** There has to be a way to help them.

    b) There might be a way to help them.

2. **a)** They must have been busy shopping for a new house.

    b) They may have been busy shopping for a new house.

3. **a)** He may have been sick.

    b) He must have been sick.

4. **a)** Your parents are going to be a little late.

    b) Your parents could be a little late.

5. **a)** She may be tired by now.

    b) She has to be tired by now.

Answers to Selected Exercises

B.
1.	The packet **may** be coming in the mail this week.	Possibility	E
2.	This nonsense **has to** stop right now.	Necessity/Instruction	DE
3.	If he **can't** do it I don't know who **can.**	Ability	DY
4.	You **may** come in.	Permission	DE
5.	O.k., fine, I **will** do it.	Promise	DY
6.	I **could have** come to the party if I knew the address.	Possibility	E
7.	You **need to** ask before taking your dad's car.	Advice	DE
8.	No one **was able to** tell what happened.	Ability	DY
9.	You **must** use a different approach to solve the problem.	Instruction	DE
10.	You **shouldn't have** taken your dad's car without permission.	Advice	DE
11.	He **is not going to** give you a raise, no matter what you do.	Willingness	DY
12.	I hear voices inside. There **must** be someone in the house.	Possibility	E

C. Sample contexts for each sentence are provided below:

1. **a)** There has to be a way to help them **get the compensation they are entitled to.**
   b) **I'm not sure what exactly we can do, but** there might be a way to help them.
2. **a)** **They told me they received an inheritance from their uncle.** They must have been busy shopping for a new house.
   b) **We haven't seen them since they won the lottery.** They may have been busy shopping for a new house, **or they may have gone on a cruise ship vacation.**
3. a) **He didn't show up at the meeting last night.** He may have been sick.
   b) **He always comes to these meetings but he didn't show up last night.** He must have been sick.
4. **a)** Your parents are going to be a little late. **They just called and told me they are caught in traffic.**
   b) **I heard there's a lot of construction on the highway.** Your parents could be a little late.
5. a) **She's been up since 5:00 a.m.** She may be tired by now.
   b) **I can't believe she cleaned the whole house this morning.** She has to be tired by now.

Constructing Noun Phrases

Every noun phrase must have at least one noun or pronoun, which is its *head.* The other words in the NP are called attributes. They may indicate the definiteness of the head, quantify it, or provide other descriptive information about it. In English, most attributes precede the head, and if there are several attributes, only certain word orders are grammatical. Determiners, for example, come first.

Types of Attributes

1. **Determiner (Det)**
   a) Articles

      DefArt: the
      IndefArt: a, an

   b) Demonstrative Determiners (DemonD)

      this, that, these, those

   c) Possessive Pronoun Determiners (PossProD)

      my, your, his, her, its, our, their

   d) Numbers

      Cardinal numbers (CardN): one, two, three
      Ordinal numbers (OrdN): first, second, next, last

   e) Pre-Articles (PreArt)

      quantifiers: all (of), some (of), neither (of)
      partitives: a pound of, a slice of
      multipliers: once, twice

2. Genitive Nouns (GenN)

3. Adjectives (Adj)

These are of several types, including those indicating size *(big, small)*, shape *(round, square)*, colour *(blue, red)*, and temperature *(hot, cool)*. Proper adjectives (a *French* restaurant) are generally capitalized. (We will simply label these *Adj.*) Of course there are many other possibilities.

4. Nouns (N)

Nouns can modify other nouns. All of the following are N N structures.

    telephone directory
    aircraft commander
    laundry detergent

5. Modifiers That Follow the Noun

    a) Postnominal modifiers (PostN)

        all, both, each
        e.g., Emma and Max both left for London last night.

    b) Prepositional phrases (PP)

        e.g., the boy in the blue shirt . . .

    c) Others; e.g., Relative Clauses, Participial Phrases, etc.

        e.g., the boy who wrote the letter . . .

Things You Need to Know About
Noun Phrases

The Noun Phrase consists of at least one element, which can be a noun *(boys)*, a personal pronoun *(he)*, an indefinite pronoun *(someone)*, and a reflexive pronoun *(himself)*, and is called **the head of the NP.** Stated differently, NP slots can be filled by nouns or personal, reflexive, and indefinite pronouns.

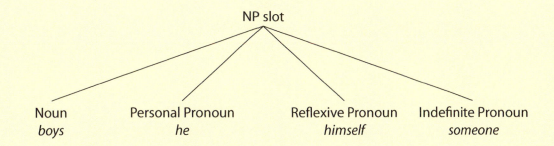

Nouns can be classified in different ways (see Ch. 2). Nouns can be:

■   **common** *(girl)* or **proper** (referring to unique people, places, or things; e.g., *Ann, the US*).
■   **concrete** *(chair)* or **abstract** *(honesty)*.
■   **countable** *(boys)* or **non-countable** *(gold)*.
■   **collective** *(flock)* or **noncollective** *(goose)*.

Noun classes overlap (e.g., *jury* is common, countable, concrete, and collective).

Personal Pronouns:

■   have **subject forms** *(I, you, he, . . .* as in *He arrived last night)* and **object forms** *(me, you, him, . . .* as in *The officer arrested him)*.
■   refer to previously mentioned nouns (shared information).
■   are used independently, instead of nouns in their slots.

Reflexive Pronouns:

■   refer to the subject of the clause they are in (e.g., ***The little boy*** *wrote his name by* ***himself***).

■   **cannot** be subjects; e.g., *Himself wrote his name.
■   when reflexive pronouns are in DO slots, the sentences can't be made passive; e.g.,

   (a)   The soccer player put **himself** in this situation.   [VT + DO]
   (b)   *Himself** was put in this situation by the soccer player.
   (c)   The soccer player called **himself** the best goalie in the country.   [Vc + DO + NP: OC].

■   look like PredN-s of VL verbs; e.g., *himself* in (a), especially because such sentences cannot be made passive (as shown in (b)), but *himself* is the DO of the VT *put* in (a) and the DO of the Vc verb *called* in (c).

Things You Need to Know About

Noun Phrases

Indefinite Pronouns:

- unlike personal and reflexive pronouns, indefinite pronouns do **not** refer to specific nouns; they are indefinite or general.
- end with -body, -thing, or -one (e.g., somebody, something, someone).

The noun phrase can be expanded with **determiners, genitives,** and **adjectives** to the left of the noun, or various **post-nominal modifiers,** ranging from single words *(all, both)* to phrases and clauses (e.g., PP, InfP, PartP, RelCl, etc.), to the right of the noun.

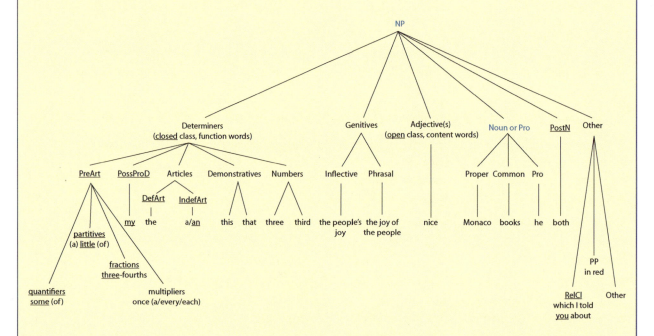

Definite articles and demonstratives:

- indicate old (known/shared/given) information; e.g., *We saw Avatar last night. Have you seen **that** movie?*
- **indefinite articles** do not express such information; e.g., *I need **a** pen.*
- **demonstratives** like *this/these* and *that/those* also point at things (the grammatical concept of pointing is called DEIXIS; it is also expressed by words like *here* and *there, now* and *then, come* and *go,* etc.).

Possessive pronouns:

- can be determiners when they precede a noun; e.g., *my car;*
- or independent possessive pronouns which fill NP slots; e.g., *This car is not **mine*** (NP:PredN); *This car is Jack's. **Mine** is in the garage* (NP:Subj).

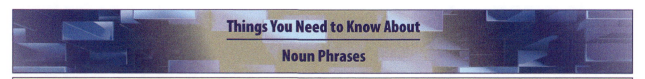

Things You Need to Know About

Noun Phrases

Numbers:

- which precede nouns are determiners; e.g., **_seven_** computers, the **_first_** computer;
- they fall into two categories:

    - **Cardinal Numbers:** *one, two, three,* etc., and
    - **Ordinal Numbers:** *first, second, third, . . . next, last.* Ordinal numbers generally follow articles as in *the **third** time around,* or possessives as in *my **second** wife.*

- Numbers that do **not** precede nouns are generally considered **nouns** themselves *(**Seven** is my lucky number; She is turning **seven** in September.)*.

Pre-articles:

- precede articles in the NP. There are several kinds (Morenberg 2010:76–77):

Quantifiers	Partitives	Fractions	Multipliers
Some (of) Any (of) No None (of) Each (of) Every Either (of) Neither (of) Many (of) (A) few (of) Several (of)	(A) little (of) Plenty (of) A lot (of) A good deal of A small quantity of An item of A slice of A bowl of A quart of A pound of A jar of	A third (of) Two-fifths (of) Three-eighths (of) . . . **Note**: when $\boxed{of}$ appears with a pre-article, it is **not** a preposition; it forms a constituent with the PreArt, not with the following noun; e.g., $\boxed{\text{a third of}}$ the students	Once (a/each/every) Twice (a/each/every) Three times (a/each/every) . . . **Note**: $\boxed{a}$, $\boxed{each}$, and $\boxed{every}$ following multipliers are determiners [*a* is the IndefArt, and *each* and *every* are **unspecified determiners**], forming a constituent first with the noun; e.g., $\boxed{once}$ a semester

Examples:

(1)   None of   my   three   dates   worked out.
     PreArt (2 wds)   PossProD   CardN   N   VI (2 wds)

(2)   Several of   the   books   I   read   gave   me   an   answer.
     PreArt (2 wds)   DefArt   N   Pro   VT   Vg   Pro   IndefArt   N

(3)   ? The   several   books   I   read   didn't   give   me   an   answer.
     DefArt   ? PreArt   N   Pro   VT   Aux+Neg   Vg   Pro   IndefArt   N

Things You Need to Know About

Noun Phrases

Genitives:

- occur as:

  (a) **inflected forms;** e.g., ***The students'*** *task is to master the six verb types,* and/or
  (b) **PPs with the Prep** *of;* e.g., *The task **of the students** is to master the six verb types;*

- usually phrasal genitives can be turned into inflected genitive; e.g., *the surface of the table,* and *the table's surface,* but there are exceptions; e.g., *my friend's leg,* but ?**the leg of my friend;*
- these forms should be called genitives rather than possessives because often they do not indicate possession at all (see Ch. 3);
- sometimes when an N is moved from a PP to the front of the head noun, the moved N won't inflect; e.g., *symbols of **identity**,* but ***identity** symbols* (see NN combinations above);
- a genitive phrase can be ambiguous about semantic roles; i.e., who performs the action and who is acted upon; e.g., *the shooting of the hunters* can be interpreted as (i) hunters shot someone, or (ii) someone shot the hunters;
- there is a difference between "of" in:

  (a) ***few of the people***, where *few of* is a PreArt (2 wds) and *people* is the head of the NP, and
  (b) ***the dream of the people***, where *dream* is the head noun, and the preposition *of* introduces a PP: Gen (synonymous to *the people's dream*).

Post-Noun Modifiers:

- appear after the noun, and can be single words; e.g., ***both**, **each**,* and ***all**;* e.g., *The teachers all/both expected this to happen.*
- however, these words can appear before the nouns (as determiners/pre-noun modifiers); e.g., *All/both (of the) teachers expected this to happen.*
- post-noun modifiers can be phrases or clauses such as PP, InfPh, RelCl, NCL (all of which are discussed in detail in later chapters); e.g.:

  - *the lady **in the red dress*** (PP),
  - *the conference **which I told you about*** (RelCl),
  - *the most important thing **to remember*** (InfPh), and
  - *it is general knowledge **that the Moon has phases*** (NCL).

Exercises

A. Identify the function of each of the underlined words using the symbols below:

Adj	N
CardN	None
CoordConj	OrdN
Correl	IndPossPro
DefArt	PossProD
DemonD	PostN
DemonPro	PreArt
Det	Prep
GenN	PropN
IndefArt	

a) **1.** <u>Both</u> <u>parents</u> worried that <u>their</u> <u>child</u> did not talk too much.

   2. <u>Both</u> <u>of</u> <u>the</u> <u>parents</u> worried that their child did not talk too much.

   3. <u>The</u> <u>parents</u> <u>both</u> worried that their child did not talk too much.

   4. I bought <u>two</u> <u>books</u> from the bookstore yesterday. <u>Both</u> are very expensive.

   5. <u>Both</u> <u>Max</u> <u>and</u> <u>his</u> <u>girlfriend</u> took part in the competition.

b) **6.** <u>The</u> <u>students</u> <u>each</u> got an award.

   7. <u>Each</u> <u>student</u> got an award.

   8. <u>Each</u> <u>of</u> <u>the</u> <u>students</u> got an award.

   9. <u>Twice</u> <u>each</u> <u>year</u> they visit Montreal.

   10. <u>Each</u> <u>year</u>, the students are randomly distributed into <u>three</u> <u>classes</u> <u>of</u> <u>twenty-five</u> <u>students</u> <u>each</u>.

c) **11.** This private gathering took place **twice a year** at Lily's home.

12. The inspector looked at **the last piece of evidence** with disbelief.

13. No one ever learned that the stolen car was **his.**

14. Maya looked at **that funny picture of a baby** and couldn't believe it was her.

15. Lady Gaga is **the new queen of pop music.**

16. As a teacher, you have to be able to understand that **each student** learns differently.

17. Thompson finished **third** in the race.

18. Most people spend **a good deal of time** thinking about nothing.

B. Decide if the underlined word in each of the following sentences is **part of a PreArt**. If it is **not** a part of a PreArt, write down what it is.

1. **An** ounce of gold, silver, or platinum can, for **a** variety

of reasons, cost either more or less than another ounce

of the same metal in the same market.

[from "Why an Ounce of Gold . . . ," goldprice.org]

1. _____

_____

2. There has been **an** unusual occurrence **of** spiders in

Florida.

[from "An Unusual Occurrence . . . ," ingentaconnect.com]

2. _____

_____

3. They will discuss how to start investing with **a** small

amount of money.

3. _____

_____

4. The book describes the greatest engineering achievements

of the twentieth century.

[adapted from greatachievements.org]

4. _____

_____

5. Please leave the last piece **of** cake for your brother.

5. _____

_____

6. **Some** portions **of** this file cannot be played.

6. _____

_____

7. Only **five** of these two hundred students got an "A."

7. _____

_____

Answers to Exercises

A. a) 1. Both   parents...   their   child
PreArt   N   PossProD   N

2. Both of   the   parents
PreArt (2 wds)   DefArt   N

3. The   parents   both
DefArt   N   PostN

4. Two   books
CardN   N
Both
N

5. Both   Max   and   his   girlfriend
Correl *(both)*   PropN   Correl *(and)*   PossProD   N

b) 6. The   students   each
DefArt   N   PostN

7. Each   student
PreArt   N

8. Each of   the   students
PreArt (2 wds)   DefArt   N

9. Twice   each   year
PreArt   Det   N

10. Each   year
PreArt   N
Three classes of   twenty-five   students   each
PerArt (3 wds)   CardN   N   PostN

c) 11. Twice   a   year
PreArt   IndefArt   N

12. The   last piece of   evidence
DefArt   PreArt (3 wds)   N

13. His
IndPossPro

14. That   funny   picture   of   a   baby
DemonD   Adj   N   Prep   IndefArt   N

15. The   new   queen   of   pop   music
DefArt   Adj   N   Prep   N   N

16. Each   student
PreArt   N

17. Third
N

18. a good deal of   time
PreArt (4 wds)   N

B.
1. <u>An</u> ounce of gold, silver, or platinum can, for <u>a</u> variety of reasons, cost either more or less than another ounce of the same metal in the same market.

2. There has been <u>an</u> unusual occurrence <u>of</u> spiders in Florida.

3. They will discuss how to start investing with <u>a</u> small amount of money.

4. The book describes the greatest engineering achievements <u>of</u> the twentieth century.

5. Please leave the last piece <u>of</u> cake for your brother.

6. <u>Some</u> portions <u>of</u> this file cannot be played.

7. Only <u>five</u> of these two hundred students got an "A."

1. Part of a PreArt (an ounce of)
Part of a PreArt (a variety of)

2. IndefArt
Prep (of)

3. Part of a PreArt (a small amount of)

4. Prep

5. Part of a PreArt (the last piece of)

6. Part of a PreArt (portions of)

7. Part of a PreArt (five of)

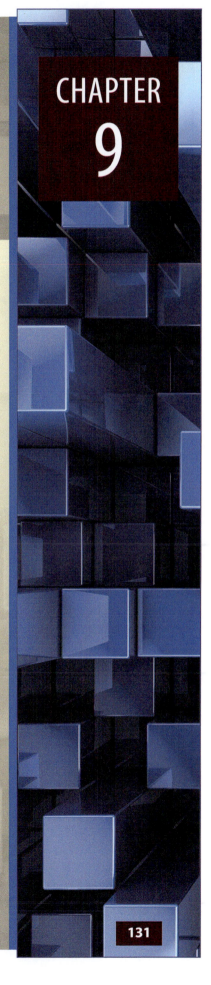

Negation

To build a negative construction out of an affirmative one, you must add the NEG marker ("not"). The general rule to remember is that if the MV is not BE or does not contain an Aux or Modal, you must also add an Aux (some form of *do*). The addition of *do* is called *do-support*.

With BE as a simple MV, insert NEG after BE.

The cat **is** lazy.	The cat **is not** lazy.	The cat **isn't** lazy.
Liz **was** a teacher.	Liz **was not** a teacher.	Liz **wasn't** a teacher.

When one or more Auxs are already present because of the perfective or progressive aspect, or the passive voice, insert NEG after the first AUX.

Joan **has** left.	Joan **has not** left.	Joan **hasn't** left.
Alan **is** writing a screenplay.	Alan **is not** writing a screenplay.	Alan **isn't** writing a screenplay.
Ken **has been** living in Regina.	Ken **has not been** living in Regina.	Ken **hasn't been** living in Regina.
The barn **was** struck by lightning.	The barn **was not** struck by lightning.	The barn **wasn't** struck by lightning.

When a modal is already present, insert NEG after the modal, but before other auxiliaries.

Mark **can** read Hebrew.	Mark **cannot** read Hebrew.	Mark **can't** read Hebrew.
Karen **should have** visited us.	Karen **should not have** visited us.	Karen **shouldn't have** visited us.

With simple verbs other than BE, add the appropriate form of DO and then NEG.

Sam **likes** Scotch.	Sam **does not like** Scotch.	Sam **doesn't like** Scotch.
Carol **ate** the apple.	Carol **did not eat** the apple.	Carol **didn't eat** the apple.

With simple catenatives, add the appropriate form of DO and then NEG.

Diane **has to** leave.	Diane **does not have to** leave.	Diane **doesn't have to** leave.
Mike **needs to** rest.	Mike **does not need to** rest.	Mike **doesn't need to** rest.

Things You Need to Know About
Negation

- If the MV is BE or contains an Aux or Modal, you must add the NEG marker "not" after BE or the first Aux/Modal:

  (a) *He is in the office.*

     not

     *He is **not** in the office.*

  (b) *He has been in the office a lot lately.*

     not

     *He has **not** been in the office a lot lately.*

- If the MV is **not** BE or does **not** contain an Aux or Modal, you must first add an Aux (some form of *do*), put it in the tense of the original verb, and then add the NEG marker "not":

  (c) *She studied Japanese in high school.*

     1. Add "do" in the appropriate form

     2. Change to past tense "did" and change "studied" to "study".

     3. Insert "not" after Aux-DO.

     *She did **not** study Japanese in high school.*

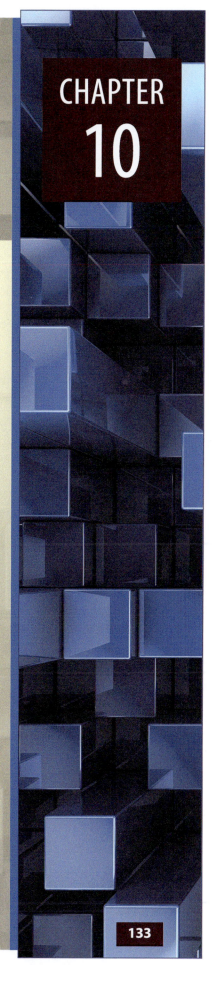

Interrogation

Forming questions out of indicative sentences involves some of the same procedures as negation. The main rule to remember is that if the MV of the indicative sentence contains no Aux, Modal, or BE, do-support is typically required.

1. Yes/No Questions

To construct yes/no interrogatives out of indicative sentences, you must move the Aux, Modal, or BE (usually with NEG, if it is present) to the beginning of the sentence.

Everyone **is** waiting for Andrew.	**Is** everyone waiting for Andrew?
Jeff **can** skate well	**Can** Jeff skate well?
The party **hasn't** begun.	**Hasn't** the party begun?
	(cf. **Has** the party **not** begun?)
Gates **is** a billionaire.	**Is** Gates a billionaire?

If the sentence does not contain an Aux, Modal, or BE, you must add one. With declarative sentences containing simple MVs other than BE and those containing catenatives, put the appropriately-tensed form of DO at the beginning of the sentence and change the MV or catenative to its base form.

Steve Jobs **detests** Microsoft.	**Does** Steve Jobs **detest** Microsoft?
The Daily Show **won** an Emmy.	**Did** *The Daily Show* **win** an Emmy?
He **has to** take a stand.	**Does** he **have to** take a stand?

2. WH-Questions

WH-questions require WH-words as shown in the next table. Unless the interrogated unit is NP:Subj, they also require the addition of the appropriate form of 'do' when no Aux, Modal, or BE is present in the MV. Note that the WH-word generally appears at the beginning of the interrogative, followed by the Aux, Modal, or BE.

There are three types of WH-words:

Interrogative Pronoun (IntPro): replaces a NP.
Interrogative Pro-Adverb (IntProAdv): replaces an adverbial unit (Adv, PP:Adv,
      NP:Adv or infinitive phrase functioning as an adverbial).
Interrogative Pro-Determiner (IntProD): replaces a determiner.

The following chart summarizes the possible wh-question types.

Interrogated phrase or word	WH-word	Role of WH-word	Example	
NP (human)	IntPro **who**	NP: Subj*	**Jim** sits in the back.	**Who** sits in the back?
	IntPro **who(m)**	NP: DO	You saw **Jim.**	**Who(m)** did you see?
	IntPro **who(m)**	NP: IO	Maureen gave the package to **Don.**	**Who(m)** did Maureen give the package to?

*Do-support is not required when the interrogated unit is the NP:Subj.

Interrogated phrase or word	WH-word	Role of WH-word	Example	
NP (non-human)	IntPro **what**	NP: Subj*	**The candle** sits on the mantle.	**What** sits on the mantle?
		NP: DO	She saw **a UFO.**	**What** did she see?
	IntPro **which**	NP: DO	He picked **the green one.**	**Which** did he pick?
Adv (time)	IntProAdv **when**	Adverbial	She left **at two.**	**When** did she leave?
Adv (manner)	IntProAdv **how**	Adverbial	He left **quietly.**	**How** did he leave?
Adv (place)	IntProAdv **where**	Adverbial	She lives **in Burnaby.**	**Where** does she live?
Adv (frequency)	IntProAdv **how often**	Adverbial	She exercises **twice a week.**	**How often** does she exercise?
Adv (reason)	IntProAdv **why**	Adverbial	She called him **to hear his voice.**	**Why** did she call him?
Det	IntProD **which**	Det	She likes **this** house.	**Which** house does she like?
	IntProD **whose**	Det	He wants **your** number.	**Whose** number does he want?
	IntProD **what**	Det	I should take **the second** bus.	**What** bus should I take?

3. More on Questions

We noted above that wh-questions are generally formed by replacing interrogated units with wh-words and by moving the wh-words, along with Aux or BE, to the front of the clause. When no Aux or BE is present, *do-support* is required. However, some other commonly-occurring question types use *formulaic expressions.* The syntax of these questions is somewhat different: *do-support* is not necessary and there is no fronting of Aux or BE. Consider the structure of the following questions. Note that the material following each formulaic expression is a clause with normal word order.

a) Questions with *"how come"*

How come the door is open?
(Why is the door open?)

How come the dog won't eat his dinner?
(Why won't the dog eat his dinner?)

How come you're hiding that box under the bed?
(Why are you hiding that box under the bed?)

b) Questions with *"_____ is it that . . ."*

What is it that you need?
(What do you need?)

Why is it that you think I'm wrong?
(Why do you think I'm wrong?)

How is it that George got a raise from his stingy boss?
(How did George get a raise from his stingy boss?)

Where is it that I should turn?
(Where should I turn?)

Another type of question with different syntactic properties is the tag or tail question. To make this kind of question,

- take the first word in AUX,
- change its polarity (make it negative if it's positive, and vice versa), and
- add the subject of the sentence; if the subject is a Pro, copy the Pro; if the Subj is not a Pro, turn the NP:Subj into a Pro:

c) Tag Questions

Your cousin is coming tomorrow, isn't she?
Your cousin isn't coming tomorrow, is she?

Things You Need to Know About
Interrogation

Yes-No Questions:

- Move the **MV BE** or the first **Aux or Modal of a MV** to the front of the sentence, unless the first word is a verb.

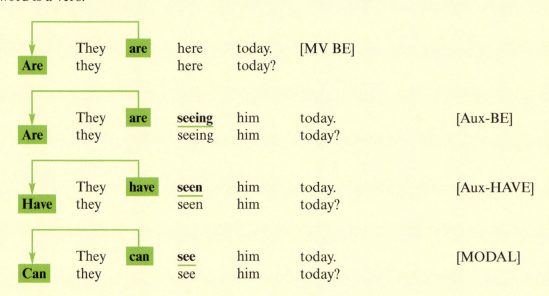

	They	**are**	here	today.	[MV BE]
Are	they		here	today?	
	They	**are**	**seeing**	him	today.	[Aux-BE]
Are	they		seeing	him	today?	
	They	**have**	**seen**	him	today.	[Aux-HAVE]
Have	they		seen	him	today?	
	They	**can**	**see**	him	today.	[MODAL]
Can	they		see	him	today?	

- There are **no changes in syntactic roles**; e.g., "they" is still the NP:Subj, "are" is MV BE, and "here" is a PredAdv in "Are they here today?"

- For all other verbs, add **DO-support** to the front of the sentence; the Aux-DO takes the tense of the verb, while the verb changes to a non-finite form (no tense).

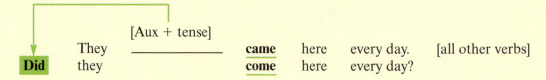

[Aux + tense]

	They	_____	**came**	here	every day.	[all other verbs]
Did	they		**come**	here	every day?	

Wh-Questions:

- They question a content phrase: usually an NP or an AdvP
- Replace an NP with an **Interrogative Pronoun** (what, who, whom), an AdvP with an **Interrogative Proadverb** (where, when, why, how, how often, etc.), and a determiner with an **Interrogative Prodeterminer** (whose, which, what)

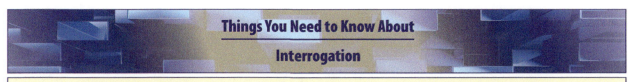

Things You Need to Know About

Interrogation

Interrogative Pronouns	Interrogative Proadverbs	Interrogative Prodeterminers
What	Where	Whose
Who	When	Which
Whom	Why	What
	How	
	How often	
	. . .	

- When the **IntPro** replaces an **NP:Subject,** no changes in the word order are made:

They laughed at my enthusiasm.   [IntPro for NP:Subj]

Who laughed at my enthusiasm?

- When the **IntPro** replaces a **non-subject NP;** e.g., DO, the IntPro has to be moved to the front together with the verb BE, a Modal, Aux-HAVE, or Aux-BE, that's already in the sentence. If none of these is already in the sentence, we have to add an Aux-DO. The Aux-DO takes the tense of the verb, while the verb changes to a non-finite form.

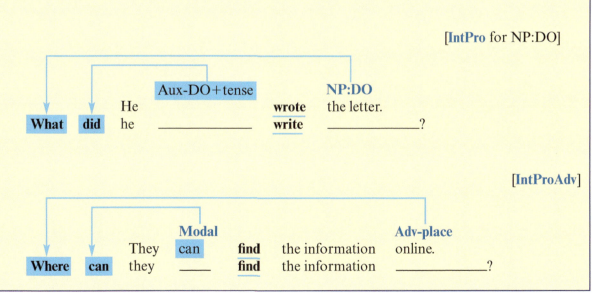

Things You Need to Know About

Interrogation

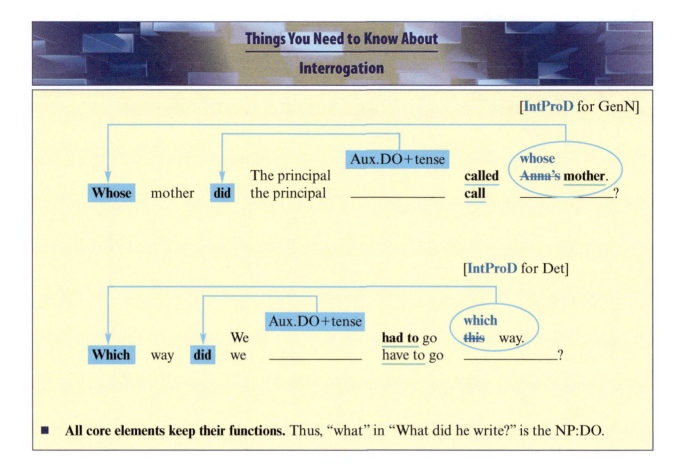

- **All core elements keep their functions.** Thus, "what" in "What did he write?" is the NP:DO.

Exercises

Parse each sentence. Then identify all of its major NPs and all PPs.

1. Why did you leave the empty bowl in the fridge?

_____

2. Where are my slippers?

_____

3. Which colour do you prefer?

_____

4. Is there a fly in your soup?

_____

5. The fly in my soup is dead.

_____

6. What do you think about this painting?

_____

7. Which side of the bed do you sleep on?

_____

8. Who is in charge here?

_____

9. What are we having for dinner?

_____

10. How much will you pay for this car?

_____

Answers to Exercises

NPs are in blue, PPs are in square brackets.

1. Why did **you** leave **the empty bowl** [in **the fridge**]_{PP:Adv}?
   IntProAdv   Aux   Pro   VT   DefArt   Adj   N   Prep   DefArt   N

2. Where are **my slippers?**
   IntProAdv   BE   PossProD   N

3. **Which colour** do **you** prefer?
   IntProD   N   Aux   Pro   VT

4. Is there **a fly** [in **your soup**]_{PP:Adv}?
   BE   Expl   IndefArt   N   Prep   PossProD   N

5. **The fly** [in **my soup**]_{PP:Adj} is dead.
   DefArt   N   Prep   PossProD   N   BE   Adj

6. **What** do **you** think [about **this painting**]_{PP:Adv}?
   IntPro   Aux   Pro   VT   Prep   DemonD   N

7. **Which side** [of **the bed**]] do **you** usually sleep [on?
   IntProD   N   Prep   DefArt   N   Aux   Pro   Adv   VI   Prep

   Note: The sentence-final "on" is the head of the PP "on which side of the bed".

8. **Who** is [in **charge**] here?
   IntPro   BE   Prep   N   Adv

9. **What** are **we** having [for **dinner**]?
   IntPro   Aux   Pro   VT   Prep   N

10. **How much**[1] will **you** pay [for **this car**]?
    IntPro (2 wds)   Modal   Pro   VT   Prep   DemonD   N

[1]"How much" is best analyzed as a single interrogative pronoun consisting of two words. In this sentence it functions as the DO of "pay."

Passives, Expletives, Imperatives, and Compounds

Passive Sentences

We discussed passive structures briefly in Chapter 4 with respect to verb types and verb complements, more specifically direct and indirect objects. In this chapter we look at the formation of the passive.

Active sentences can be made passive by moving an object into a subject position, and making the verb passive with the help of AuxBE and the past participle form of the verb. This process is called passivization.

The AuxBE takes the tense of the active verb; i.e., if the active verb is past (e.g., wrote), the passive form of the verb contains AuxBE in the past tense and past participle form of the verb.

Active Julianne Marsh **wrote** the novel in 1963.
Passive The novel **was written** in 1963 (by Julianne Marsh).

This is done when the doer of the action is unknown or irrelevant; e.g., when it is more important when the novel was written rather than who wrote it.

Expletive Sentences

Two of the most common types of expletive sentences contain words with primarily grammatical function such as:

a) **Existential "there"**; e.g., **There** are three yogurts in the fridge.
b) **"It"-expletives**; e.g., **It** is time to go; **It**'s cold today.

Existential-*there* structures can often be derived from sentences with the MV BE and an Adv-place; e.g., sentence (a) could be derived from "Three yogurts are in the fridge," by inserting "there" in the subject slot, and moving the original subject ("three yogurts") in the PredN position. In the new structure, "there" is the Grammatical Subject, while the PredN continues to be the topic or agent, so it is the Logical Subject.

In sentences containing *it*-expletives, the word "it" is **not** a pronoun and does **not** refer to a previously-mentioned noun. It simply fills in the grammatical slot of a subject. Compare "it" in sentence (b), and "it" in a sentence like:

I bought **a new TV** yesterday. **It** is big.   **NOT** an Expletive *it* structure.

Here, "it" clearly refers to and replaces the NP "a new TV," so it is a pronoun.

Similar to existential-*there,* expletive **it** is the Grammatical Subject, while the PredN or PredAdj following the verb BE is the Logical Subject.

A third type of expletive is Aux-DO, because the function of DO-support is purely grammatical; i.e., to make a sentence negative, turn it into a question, etc., as in (c):

c) **Aux-DO;** e.g., Why **does**n't he have time?

Note, however, that we use the label Aux-DO, not Expl.

Imperatives

Linguists argue that imperatives are derived from sentences with *You:* Subj and Modal-*Will* as (a), where the subject and the Aux both get deleted as shown in (b), and the result is (c):

a) You will give me this book.   Underlying structure
b) ~~You will~~ give me this book.   Deletion of Subj + Aux
c) **Give me this book!**   Surface Structure

As a result, the imperative is the only sentence type in English which can occur **without a subject** in the surface structure (c), though the implied subject in this example is the addressee—singular or plural you. Occasionally the subject "you" is retained for emphasis; e.g.,

d) Hey, **you,** give me this book!

Note that there can be first-person plural imperatives (e.g., "Let's go!"), and third-person imperatives (e.g., "Let there be light!", "God Bless You!", and "Politicians be damned!").

The imperative is the only sentence type in English **without tense** (because when we delete Aux, we delete tense with it, and the verb is in infinitive form).

Compound Structures (Cpd)

Similar or identical structures (phrases or clauses) can be joined together with the help of two main types of conjunctions—coordinating and correlative. A third type of conjunctions—subordinating—join an independent/main clause and its dependent/

subordinate clause(s). We introduced these conjunctions in Chapter 2. Here is a quick review:

Coordinating Conjunctions	and, or, so, but . . . e.g., *She left, and he started crying.*
Correlative Conjunctions	neither . . . nor . . . , either . . . or . . . , not only . . . but also . . . e.g., *Neither the children nor their parents understood the new rules.*
Subordinating Conjunctions	if, after, when, because, since . . . (under some circumstances) e.g., *You can go out after you finish your homework.*

Coordinating conjunctions can join individual words or phrases, or clauses (as shown in examples (1)-(4) below), correlative conjunctions usually join NPs (as in (5)), and subordinating conjunctions join only clauses (as in (6)). If the same words that can function as subordinating conjunctions are followed by phrases; e.g., PPs as in "after dinner," they are called prepositions, not conjunctions (as in (7)).

1)	Jane, Lucas **and** Emma went home.	CoordConj	Cpd N-s:Subj-s
2)	I saw the boy **and** his dog.	CoordConj	Cpd NP-s:DO-s
3)	I saw the boy **and** smiled.	CoordConj	Cpd VP-s
4)	They saw me, **and** the dog barked cheerfully.	CoordConj	Cpd Sentences
5)	**Neither** Jane **nor** Lucas wanted to go home.	Correl	NP-s: Subj-s
6)	**After** I finished my homework, I went out.	SubordConj	introducing an AdvCl
7)	**After** dinner, I went out.	Prep	followed by NP "dinner"

Things You Need to Know About

Passives, Expletives, Imperatives, and Compounds

Passives

There are **multiple steps involved in passivization.** The first four steps are obligatory, while the last three are optional.

(1) Move NP:Obj (DO or IO) before the V into the Subj. slot, so it becomes the Grammatical Subject;

(2) Introduce BE into Aux;

(3) Add TENSE to BE in Aux;

(4) Change verb into PastPart form;

(5) Add a PP: Adv-agency with Prep "by" (optional—could be omitted altogether);

(6) Move the NP:Subj of the active sentence into PP with "by"; it becomes Obj/Prep "by" and is also the Logical Subject (this step is conditional on step 5);

(7) If the NP:Subj in the active is a Pronoun, change it from Subj to Obj form after the Prep "by" (e.g., "He" → "by him").

■ Note **that agency and semantic roles; i.e., who does what to whom, are preserved** in passives:

■ hence NP:Obj/Prep remains the doer of the action (or the giver with Vg verbs) or the Logical Subject,

■ the DO remains the affected entity or the entity acted upon, though it may show up as the Gram. Subject, or retain its DO status (as in "He was given the disc last night"), and

■ the IO (if any) remains the receiver.

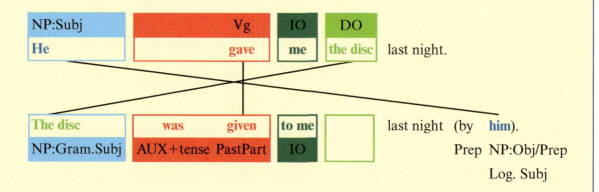

■ Passives can be made from sentences with **one- or two-place transitive verbs only;** i.e., VT, Vg, and Vc verbs.

■ However, **not all sentences with transitive verbs can be made passive;** e.g., My car costs a fortune. vs. *A fortune is cost by my car. The exceptions involve verbs like *cost, weigh, have,* and *resemble.*

■ **Important Note: the easiest way to analyze passive sentences, especially their verbs, is to turn them back into active.** Thus, the easiest way to see that "elected" is a Vc verb in "He was elected president twice" is to turn it back into active and see that it is followed both by a DO "him" and an OC "president."

Things You Need to Know About

Passives, Expletives, Imperatives, and Compounds

He	**was elected**	____	president	twice	____ .

____ (by the people).

They/the people	**elected**	**him**	president	twice.
NP:Subj	Vc	NP: DO	NP: OC	

- **The PP with "by" is often deleted** when the information is irrelevant, unknown, or old (shared information).

  Taxes will be increased again ~~by the government~~ this summer.
  [Assumed to be shared knowledge].

- **Past participles and adjectives can look alike;** e.g., "The doctor was annoyed" can be analyzed as (a) "someone; e.g., his patients, annoyed the doctor" (passive, where "was" is Aux, and "annoyed" is PastPart); or as (b) "the doctor was in a state of annoyance" (active, where "was" is MV BE, and "annoyed" is PredAdj; similar to the "doctor was angry"). When in doubt, indicate both possible interpretations:

	The	doctor	was	annoyed.
(a)	DefArt	N	Aux-Be	VT
(b)	DefArt	N	BE	Adj

- **Passives can be made negative or turned into questions:**

  The wallet **has been found.**
  The wallet **has not been found.**
  Has the wallet **been found?**
  Hasn't the wallet **been found?**
  When was the wallet **found?**
  Where was the wallet **found?**

- There are **progressive, perfect, and conditional passives,** and combinations of them too:

The book **is being made** into a movie.	Present progressive passive
The book **had been made** into a movie.	Past perfect passive
The book **must have been made** into a movie.	Past perfect conditional passive

- **"GET" can be used as an Aux instead of "BE" in passives:**

  He **was robbed** by this own family.

  He **got robbed** by his own family.   (especially frequent in informal American English).

Things You Need to Know About

Passives, Expletives, Imperatives, and Compounds

Expletives

- **An expletive** is a word that **has a grammatical function,** but **no meaning** of its own.
- The most common types of expletive constructions contain **existential-*there*** or **expletive *it*,** functioning as the **Grammatical Subject.**
- A MV BE + Adv-place:PredAdv can often be rearranged into an **existential-there** sentence.

- The **NP:Subj** of the core sentence is moved **after the verb BE** and is the PredN (and retains its semantic role, hence it is also the **Logical Subject**).

- The word **"there"** is placed into the now empty subject slot and becomes a **Grammatical Subject.**

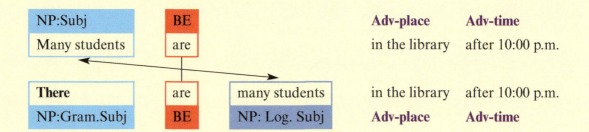

- **Expletive *it*** also occurs in subject position in constructions such as *It is sunny* and *It is natural to miss home when you live abroad,* where the word "it" is **not** a pronoun, and has a primary grammatical function. Compare also:

**Expletive *it*
Gram. Subj**

(a) **It was too dark** outside, and we couldn't see anything.
(b) The photographer didn't like that picture. **It was too dark**.

**Pronoun
Log. Subj**

"It" in (a) does **not** replace a previously-mentioned NP, and fills in the Subject slot, so it is expletive *it* and Grammatical Subject, while in (b) "it" clearly replaces the NP "that picture," so it is a pronoun and Logical Subject as well as a grammatical subject in this sentence.

- Aux-DO in negative sentences or questions is also an expletive: Aux-DO shows tense and acts like a dummy modal; e.g., **Do** you see it? We'll mark DO as Aux, not Expl.

Things You Need to Know About

Passives, Expletives, Imperatives, and Compounds

Imperatives

- These are commands or orders like "Give me the bag!"

- They have no visible subject; they have an understood or implied "you" as a subject.

- Delete "will," and most often the subject "you," in a declarative sentence to turn it into an imperative.

  ~~You will~~ give me the bag   vs.   Give me the bag!

- Imperatives can have tags, which are invariably "won't you": e.g.,

  Give me the bag, **won't you**?   [esp. in American English]

- The negative form of imperatives requires DO-support before the NEG particle "not" is inserted; e.g.,

  Do not give me the bag!
  Don't give me the bag!

Compounds

- The meaning of "compound" is "conjoin, coordinate."

- Connective words and phrases are called conjunctions.

- Two types of conjunctions are used in compounding: Coordinate and Correlative.

- **Coordinate conjunctions (CoordConj)** are single words like *and, but, or, yet,* and *so.* These can join words, phrases, and clauses.

  He was wondering if she was still awake **or** already asleep.

- **Correlative conjunctions (Correl)** are pairs of words such as both . . . and, either . . . or, neither . . . nor, not only . . . but also.

  Neither the couple **nor** their parents knew the truth about what happened.

- **A note on punctuation (though it is not grammar):** When two words or phrases are conjoined, usually there's no comma, while when three or more words or phrases are conjoined, a comma is placed between the items; e.g.,

  Mary **and** Nick

  Mary **,** Nick **, and** James   or   Mary **,** Nick **and** James

  The last example shows two types of punctuation: US-style with a comma placed between all items and Anglo-Canadian style without a comma after the penultimate NP in a series.

Things You Need to Know About

Passives, Expletives, Imperatives, and Compounds

- Also, when two or more clauses are conjoined, some punctuation is used (e.g., comma, semicolon, period + new sentence) as in:

  She loved him **,** **but** he didn't know it.

  She loved him **;** **but** he didn't know it.

  She loved him **.** **But** he didn't know it.

- Words and phrases like *besides, however, finally, moreover, to sum up,* etc. are **adverbs** which link different sentences in the discourse, hence their function is better analyzed on the paragraph and larger level, rather than on the sentence level.

- Unlike conjunctions, these adverbs can move around; e.g.,

  They promised to come. **However** , they never showed up.

  They promised to come. They never showed up, **however** .

Quick Quiz

What is the function of each underlined word?

(1) **Both** students came to my office to talk to me.   _____

(2) **Both** Mary **and** Ann came to my office to talk to me.   _____

(3) **Neither** applicant has the required qualifications.   _____

(4) **Neither** Jim **nor** Bob has the required qualifications.   _____

(5) I looked at two shirts at the store. I didn't like **either**.   _____

Exercises

A. Parse each sentence. Then identify all of its major NPs and all PPs.

   1. She had a lot of money, so she bought some new shoes.

_____

   2. He climbed on his bicycle and rode down the path.

_____

   3. Were they working or taking a break?

_____

   4. Did you tell Frank and Joe the good news?

_____

   5. Whose computer got stolen?

_____

B. Parse each sentence and then identify its voice. If it is passive, convert it to its active form. If it is active, convert it to its passive form.

   1. Marilyn sent a package of documents to Jerry.

_____

   2. Your luggage somehow got shipped to Albania.

_____

   3. The gold medal had been kept in a safe prior to the event.

_____

   4. Isn't she driving her parents crazy with her choices in music?

_____

5. Her garden was being designed by an expert.

_____

6. Haven't you been contacted by the company yet?

_____

7. Gwendolyn was awarded first prize in the school's music competition.

_____

8. Fred was throwing out the trash.

_____

9. Why didn't the mechanic replace your muffler?

_____

10. The band's new CD has been called boring.

_____

C. Are the underlined words examples of **existential-_there_** ? Reply with _Yes_ or _No_, and identify the function of the words for which you answered "No."

1. There is ice on the ground.   _____ _____

2. They have a lot of ice **there.**   _____ _____

3. And **here** comes my mom!   _____ _____

4. Here is a copy of your permit.   _____ _____

5. There's three people in the car.   _____ _____

6. He looked at **their** car.   _____ _____

7. They're in the car.   _____ _____

D. Are the underlined words expletives ? Reply with *Yes* or *No*, and identify the function of the words for which you answered "No."

1. Your bicycle is very nice. I saw **it** in the yard. _____ _____

2. I just bought this table, but **its** leg is broken. _____ _____

3. A: Who's calling?
B: **It**'s your mom. _____ _____

4. Take an umbrella! **It** is raining. _____ _____

5. She lives **here.** _____ _____

6. **Here** are my boys. _____ _____

7. **Do** you like her? _____ _____

E. Can these sentences be made passive ? Reply with *Yes* or *No*, and provide a brief explanation why.

Example: He became a doctor.
Answer: No; *become:* VL (not a transitive verb)

1. This piano weighs a ton. _____ _____

2. The principal gave him another book. _____ _____

3. Newer airplanes have more sophisticated protection against electromagnetic interference.
[from aircraftsystemsafety.com] _____ _____

4. They both arrived fifteen minutes late. _____ _____

5. We are fooling ourselves about healthy eating.
[from Are We Fooling . . . ?, facebook.com] _____ _____

6. Art reflects life with special mirrors.
[Bertolt Brecht; wikiquote.org] _____ _____

7. Students can be leaders in the fight against poverty. _____ _____

F. Can the following sentences be turned into existential *there* ? Please reply with *Yes* if a sentence can be turned into existential "there" without replacing its verb with another verb, or *No* if this cannot be done.

1. The first few months he followed his girlfriend everywhere. _____ _____

2. Your subconscious mind cannot distinguish something real from something just vividly imagined. [Secrets of Success . . . , ezinearticles.com] _____ _____

3. Terry Fox's Marathon of Hope began in 1980. [from terryfox.org] _____ _____

4. Only several hundred selected invitees were at the royal wedding on April 29, 2011. _____ _____

5. The rain stopped in the late afternoon. _____ _____

6. Seven hundred people were in the store for the grand opening. _____ _____

7. Why are so many socks on the floor? _____ _____

Extra Practice:

G. Are the underlined words instances of expletive *it* ? Reply with *Yes* or *No*, and identify the function of the words for which you answered "No."

1. At that moment Machu Picchu revealed itself to us in all **its** grandeur. [whereoneartharewe.com] _____ _____

2. **It**'s necessary to complete these forms before you sell the company. _____ _____

3. The heavy books were in a plastic bag that didn't look very reliable. **It** ripped off a few minutes after they left. _____ _____

4. **It**'s a rule of thumb to look before you leap. _____ _____

5. Music is, in **its** essence, repetition. [www.crispinsartwell.com] _____ _____

6. Is **it** mandatory for parents to assist in school projects? _____ _____

7. **It**'s recommended that you place one carbon monoxide detector on each level of your home. [stayingalive.ca]

   _____   _____

8. I made a joke and **it** backfired.

   _____   _____

9. **It**'s Canada's time to quit smoking. [itscanadastime.com]

   _____   _____

10. I don't like **it** when you get that look.

   _____   _____

Answers to the Quick Quiz:

1. PreArt
2. Correl   Correl
3. PreArt
4. Correl   Correl
5. Noun

Answers to Selected Exercises

C. Existential-*there*

1. **There** is ice on the ground.   Yes

2. They have a lot of ice **there.**   No   Adv-place

3. And **there** comes my mom!   Yes   existential *here* and *there* can occur, though rarely, with *come* and *go* as in "There goes all my money!"

4. **Here** is a copy of your permit.   Yes

5. **There's** three people in the car.   Yes   Prescriptive note: Though increasingly common in everyday spoken English, this sentence violates prescriptive rules on agreement.

6. He looked at **their** car.   No   PossProD

7. **They're** in the car.   No   Pro=NP:Subj + MV BE

D. Expletives

1. Your bicycle is very nice. I saw **it** in the yard.   No   Pro (refers to "your bicycle")

2. I just bought this table, but **its** leg is broken.   No   PossProD

3. A: Who's calling?
   B: **It**'s your mom.   Yes

4. Take an umbrella! **It** is raining.   Yes

5. She lives **here.**   No   Adv-place

6. **Here** are my boys.   Yes

7. **Do** you like her?   Yes   Aux-DO

E. Passives

1. This piano weighs a ton. **No** *weigh:* VT, but exception

2. The principal gave him another book. **Yes** *gave:* Vg

3. Newer airplanes have more sophisticated protection against electromagnetic interference. **No** *have:* VT, but exception

4. They both arrived fifteen minutes late. **No** *arrived:* VI

5. We are fooling ourselves about healthy eating. **No** reflexive Pro *ourselves* cannot be subject, → no passive

6. Art reflects life with special mirrors. **Yes** *reflects:* VT

7. Students can be leaders in the fight against poverty. **No** MV BE

F. Existential-*there*

1. The first few months he followed his girlfriend everywhere. **No** *followed:* VT

2. Your subconscious mind cannot distinguish something real from something just vividly imagined. **No** *distinguish:* VT

3. Terry Fox's Marathon of Hope began in 1980. **No** *began:* VI

4. There were only several hundred selected invitees at the royal wedding on April 29, 2011. **Yes** MV BE + Adv-place

5. The rain stopped in the late afternoon. **No** *stopped:* VI

6. There were seven hundred people in the store for the grand opening. **Yes** MV BE + Adv-place

7. Why are there so many socks on the floor? **Yes** MV BE + Adv-place

Extra Practice:

G. **Expletive** *it*

1. At that moment Machu Picchu revealed itself to us in all **its** grandeur.

> **1.** No   PossProD

2. **It**'s necessary to complete these forms before you sell the company.

> **2.** Yes

3. The heavy books were in a plastic bag that didn't look very reliable. **It** ripped off a few minutes after they left.

> **3.** No   Pro (replaces "a plastic bag")

4. **It**'s a rule of thumb to look before you leap.

> **4.** Yes

5. Music is, in **its** essence, repetition.

> **5.** No   PossProD

6. Is **it** mandatory for parents to assist in school projects?

> **6.** Yes

7. **It**'s recommended that you place one carbon monoxide detector on each level of your home.

> **7.** Yes

8. I made a joke and **it** backfired.

> **8.** No   Pro (refers to "a joke")

9. **It**'s Canada's time to quit smoking.

> **9.** Yes

10. I don't like **it** when you get that look.

> **10.** ?   This is an interesting one! Many will answer "No", because "it" is a DO, not a Subj; however, it is used in a formulaic expression, where, one could argue, it fills the slot of a dummy object.

Clause and Sentence Types

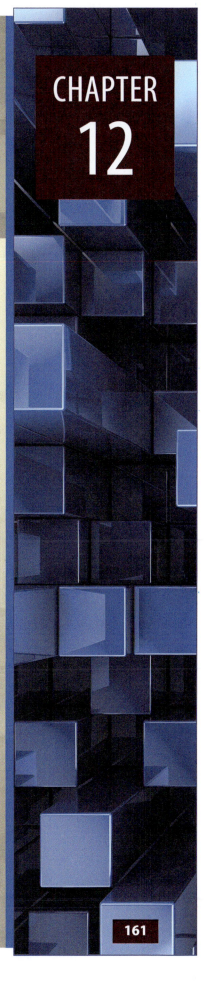

Traditionally, clauses are classified as either **independent** (those that can stand on their own as "complete ideas") or **dependent** (subordinate clauses that cannot stand alone because they depend upon another idea). A sentence may consist of a single clause or two or more clauses connected together through coordination or subordination. Traditional grammar books identify four sentence types.

Simple   *A single independent clause. Note that simple sentences can contain compound units such as compound NPs and VPs.*

The bird sang sweetly.
The sparrow and the chickadee sang sweetly.
The bird landed on a branch and sang sweetly.
The bird landed on a branch, ate a delicious caterpillar, and flew away.

Compound   *Two or more independent clauses joined by one or more coordinating conjunctions.*

The bird sang, and the bee buzzed.
The bird landed on the branch, so the caterpillar tried to crawl away.

Complex   *One independent clause with one or more dependent (subordinate) clauses.*

When the bird landed on the branch, the caterpillar tried to crawl away.
When the bird landed on the branch, the caterpillar, who had been dozing, tried to crawl away.

Compound-   *More than one independent clause accompanied by at*
Complex   *least one dependent (subordinate) clause.*
When the caterpillar moved, the bird tried to eat him, but the cat, who had been sitting on the roof, jumped down and caught the bird.

Things You Need to Know About

Sentence Types

In order to determine which clauses are dependent and which are independent, separate a sentence into clauses and see which ones can stand on their own.

A clause contains a **NP:Subject** and a **VP:Predicate;** e.g.,

My boss called me last night.

If a clause can stand on its own, it is an independent (or main) clause. If it **cannot** stand on its own, it is a dependent (or subordinate) clause.

Below are four sentences which illustrate the four sentence types, and their schematic presentations:

(1) The bird landed on a branch and sang sweetly.
(2) The bird landed on the branch, so the caterpillar tried to crawl away.
(3) When the bird landed on the branch, the caterpillar, who had been dozing, tried to crawl away.
(4) When the caterpillar moved, the bird tried to eat him, but the cat, who had been sitting on the roof, jumped down and caught the bird.

Simple and Compound Sentences
Simple and compound sentences contain only independent clauses. A simple sentence has only one independent clause, though it may have compound elements (e.g., a compound verb phrase as in sentence (1)), while a compound sentence has two or more independent clauses linked by coordinating conjunctions (2).

Sentence Type	Conjunctions	Independent Clauses
1. Simple		**(i)** the bird landed on a branch and sang sweetly. VP Conj VP
2. Compound	so	**(i)** the bird landed on the branch **(ii)** the caterpillar tried to crawl away

Complex and Compound-complex Sentences
Complex and compound-complex sentences contain at least one dependent clause. A complex sentence has only one independent clause (3), while a compound-complex sentence contains two or more independent clauses (4).

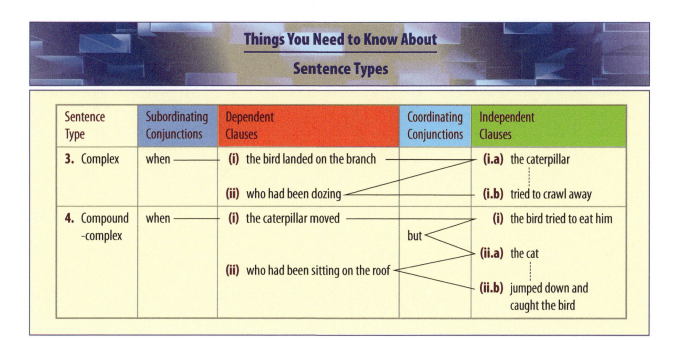

Things You Need to Know About

Sentence Types

Sentence Type	Subordinating Conjunctions	Dependent Clauses		Coordinating Conjunctions	Independent Clauses
3. Complex	when	**(i)** the bird landed on the branch			**(i.a)** the caterpillar
		(ii) who had been dozing			**(i.b)** tried to crawl away
4. Compound-complex	when	**(i)** the caterpillar moved			**(i)** the bird tried to eat him
				but	**(ii.a)** the cat
		(ii) who had been sitting on the roof			**(ii.b)** jumped down and caught the bird

Exercises

A. Determine the type of each sentence as one of the following:
   a) simple sentence
   b) compound sentence
   c) complex sentence
   d) compound-complex sentence

1. She had a lot of money, yet she only bought cheap stuff.

1. _____

2. The gold medal had been kept in a safe prior to the event.

2. _____

3. The scale of Japan's March 11 earthquake and tsunami wasn't
the only thing that surprised geologists.

[from "Japan Quake . . . ," livescience.com]

3. _____

4. Heavy sand and rocks sink, while water and lighter sand
bubble to the surface.

[from "Japan Quake . . . ," livescience.com]

4. _____

5. We've seen localized examples of soil liquefaction as extreme
as this before, but the distance and extent of damage in Japan
were unusually severe.

[from "Japan Quake . . . ," livescience.com]

5. _____

6. Researchers have yet to decide on the most vulnerable area in
the world, but Ethiopia and Bangladesh are certainly near the
top of the disaster-friendly list.

[from "Estonia: The Safest . . . ," ca.news.yahoo.com]

6. _____

7. This scrutiny will grow exponentially and extend to all aspects of Kate Middleton's life.

[adapted from royalwedding.yahoo.com]

7. _____

8. According to a recent study, women consider themselves old at twenty-nine as soon as they spot their first grey hairs, but men don't feel over the hill until the age of fifty-eight.

[from "Men Feel Old . . . ," ca.news.yahoo.com]

8. _____

9. The majority of men don't feel old until they've reached retirement age.

[from "Men Feel Old . . . ," ca.news.yahoo.com]

9. _____

10. This gulf between the sexes arises because age perception is so determined by society's attitude towards youth and beauty.

[from "Men Feel Old . . . ," ca.news.yahoo.com]

10. _____

11. In our society, men don't have to be good looking, but, for some reason, it's important for women to be attractive.

[from "Men Feel Old . . . ," ca.news.yahoo.com]

11. _____

12. On Friday, the clip still ranked as one of the top five most popular stories on USA Today's website.

12. _____

B. Underline the independent clauses, bracket the dependent clauses, and box all the subordinating and coordinating conjunctions used to link clauses in the twelve sentences from Exercise A. Remember that clauses can have compound elements; e.g., an independent clause may have a compound VP, but it still counts as one independent clause.

Answers to Exercises A and B

1. She had a lot of money, | yet | she only bought cheap stuff.

                                                                      1. compound

2. The gold medal had been kept in a safe prior to the event.

    2. simple (passive)

3. The scale of Japan's March 11 earthquake and tsunami wasn't the only thing [that surprised geologists].

    3. complex

4. Heavy sand and rocks sink, [| while | water and lighter sand bubble to the surface].

    4. complex

5. We've seen localized examples of soil liquefaction as extreme as this before, | but | the distance and extent of damage in Japan were unusually severe.

    5. compound

6. Researchers have yet to decide on the most vulnerable area in the world, | but | Ethiopia and Bangladesh are certainly near the top of the disaster-friendly list.

    6. compound

7. This scrutiny will grow exponentially and extend to all aspects of Kate Middleton's life.

    7. simple (Cpd-VP)

8. According to a recent study, women consider themselves old at twenty-nine [| as soon as | they spot their first grey hairs], | but | men don't feel over the hill until the age of fifty-eight.

    8. compound-complex

9. The majority of men don't feel old [| until | they've reached retirement age].

    9. complex

10. This gulf between the sexes arises [| because | age perception is so determined by society's attitude towards youth and beauty].

    10. complex

11. In our society, men don't have to be good looking, | but | , for some reason, it's important for women to be attractive.

    11. compound

12. On Friday, the clip still ranked as one of the top five most popular stories on USA Today's website.

    12. simple

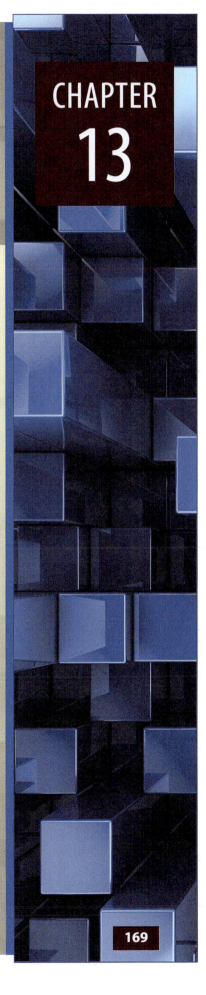

Subordinate Clauses

Noun		Chicken Little thought _{NCL} [that the sky was falling.]
		_{NCL} [What he told Turkey Lurkey] was quite frightening.
		The fact _{NCL} [that he was hysterical] soon became apparent.
Noun modifier		The house _{RELCL} [that stands on the corner] is made of straw.
		The old goose, _{RELCL}[who was swimming on the pond], became alarmed.
Adverb	(time)	_{ADVCL} [When the farmer entered the barn], the pigs stopped their poker game.
	(cause)	Red Riding Hood was frightened _{ADVCL} [because the wolf had big teeth].
	(condition)	_{ADVCL} [If you need a spinning wheel], we'll find you one.
	(concession)	_{ADVCL} [Although the wolf was tired], he tried to blow down the house.
	(manner)	The pig grunted _{ADVCL} [as though he needed food].
	(purpose)	The hen picked the wheat _{ADVCL} [so that she could make some bread].

Noun clauses, bracketed below with the label **"NCL,"** fit one of two general categories:

1. "that" clauses

Although "that clauses" begin with "that," they are not relative clauses. Instead they function as nouns and can play such roles as NP:Subj, NP:DO, or NP:PredN. Furthermore, in these structures, "that" functions as a COMP, rather than as a RelPro.

_{NCL} [That the politician is corrupt] is obvious. (NP:Subj)
He believed _{NCL} [that the truth would come out]. (NP:DO)
The trouble is _{NCL} [that the leader has no charisma]. (NP:PredN)

It is often idiomatic to extrapose noun clauses:

It is obvious _{NCL} [that the politician is corrupt].

In the example above, "it" is an Expl playing the role of grammatical subject of the sentence. The extraposed noun clause is the logical subject, but has taken the role of Comp to the Adj. "obvious." In the case below, the noun clause moves to become Comp to NP:

_{NCL} [That Joe lost the election] surprised everyone.
It surprised everyone_{NCL} [that Joe lost the election].

In many instances, COMP can be deleted:

He believed _{NCL} [that the truth would come out].
He believed _{NCL} [the truth would come out].

COMP-deletion cannot occur when the noun clause functions as NP:Subj:

_{NCL} [That he will lead the party] is obvious.
*He will lead the party is obvious.

2. Wh-clauses

These are noun clauses beginning with such wh-subordinators (WhSub) as what, who, when, where, why, whether, how, how often, and a few others.

_{NCL} [What Ken wants] is a good meal.

In the example above, **what Ken wants** functions as the NP:Subj of the sentence. Note also that within the noun clause **Ken** has the role of NP:Subj, **wants** is a VT, and **what** has the role of NP:DO.

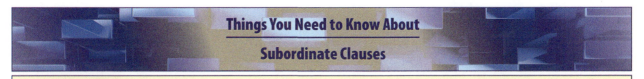

Things You Need to Know About

Subordinate Clauses

Relative Clauses

- relative clauses are dependent clauses;
- they function as Adjectives within NPs modifying the NP and narrowing down its meaning from a bigger set of referents to a smaller set and possibly a single referent
- they usually answer questions like What, Which, etc.;
- they have their own NP:Subj and VP:Pred.

In the following example, all elements of the main clause are green, while the elements of the relative clause are red.

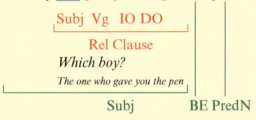

The boy **who** gave you the pen is my son.

- The Subject of the main clause is not just "the boy," but "the boy who gave you the pen"
- The NP:Subj consists of two elements:

    - Head NP ("the boy"), and
    - RelCl:Adj ("who gave you the pen")

The diagram below shows how relative clauses are embedded as dependent elements within a main clause. In this sentence, the RelCl is nested into the DO of the main clause "the man."

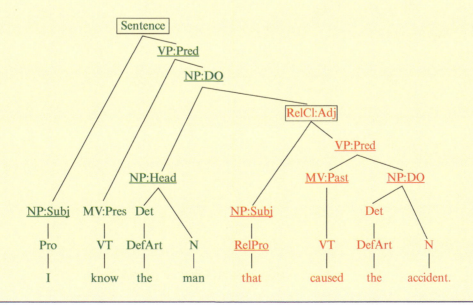

Things You Need to Know About

Subordinate Clauses

- Relative Clauses are usually introduced by relative pronouns: **who, whom, which,** and **that,** which we will label as RelPro.
- **Who** (in Subject position as in (1)) and **whom** (in Object position: DO, IO, Obj/Prep as in (2)) are used for animate NPs, **which** is used for inanimate NPs (as in (3)), and **that** can replace any of these three.
- Relative Clauses can also be introduced by other relative forms; e.g., the relative determiner **whose** (as in (4)), which we'll label RelDet, and sometimes by the words **when** and **where** (as in (5) and (6)).
- The table below illustrates some of the most frequently used relative forms:

Animate NPs		Inanimate NPs	
NP:Subj	NP:Obj (DO, IO, Obj/Prep)	Subj or Obj	PossProD or GenN
who	whom[1]	which	
that			whose

[1]**A note on Prescriptive Grammar:** Prescriptive rules require this form in object position, but as sentence (2) shows, "who" is also acceptable in informal contexts. In addition, sentence (2) may be criticized by prescriptivists because the Prep "to" is placed at the end of the RelCl rather than before the word "whom."

- Here are some examples of sentences containing RelCl:

(1) The man $\begin{bmatrix} \text{who} \\ \text{that} \end{bmatrix}$ was talking about this is a famous author.

            Subj of the RelCl (refers to a person)

(2) The man $\begin{bmatrix} \text{whom} \\ \text{who} \\ \text{that} \\ \varnothing \end{bmatrix}$ she talked to is her dad.

            Obj/Prep "to" (refers to a person)

(3) It was one of these things $\begin{bmatrix} \text{which} \\ \text{that} \\ \varnothing \end{bmatrix}$ she hated to do.

            DO in the RelCl (refers to an inanimate NP)

(4) (a) She worked with kids **whose** parents were in prison.

            RelDet (replaces a GenN or a PossProD)

Things You Need to Know About

Subordinate Clauses

(5) The town ⌈where ⌉I was born was the host of the 1988 Olympic Games.
         ⌊in which⌋

(6) The day when he got the award was one of the most memorable days in his life.

- The RelPro can be deleted when it does **not** function as the subject of its own clause. For example, the RelPro "that" can be deleted in (2) and (3) but not in (1), because in (2) and (3) it is in Object position, while in (1) it is in Subject position.

- Compare also (1) and (7). In (7) the RelPro is the Object of the preposition "about" in the RelCl (note that "he" is the Subj of the RelCl), hence it can be deleted, while in (1) (repeated as (8)) it is the Subj of the RelCl, and cannot be deleted.

(7) The man **that** he was talking about is a famous author.
         The man ___ he was talking about is a famous author.
                  |
              Obj/Prep "about" in the RelCl

(8)   The man **that** was talking about this is a famous author.
          *The man ___ was talking about this is a famous author.
                   |
               Subj in the RelCl

- Multiple relative clauses can be embedded into one another. In sentence (9), for example, the RelCl "that he recommended to the lady who was singing in the piano bar," modifying "the book," has another RelCl embedded into it, "who was singing in the piano bar," modifying "the lady":

(9) She bought **the book** that he recommended to **the lady** who was singing in the piano bar.
                                                                                RelCl 1
                                                     RelCl 2

Things You Need to Know About

Subordinate Clauses

Noun Clauses

- Noun clauses (NCL) always fill noun slots.

- There are two types of Noun clauses: That-clauses and Wh-Clauses.

- That Clauses are introduced by the so-called complementizer "that," labeled as COMP (it is also called a Subordinating conjunction, and a Subordinator, labeled as Subord).

- The COMP "that" only introduces or signals the beginning of a that-clause; it does **not** have a grammatical function in the subordinate clause.
- That-clauses fulfill various functions; they can be subjects, direct objects, predicate nouns, complements to adjectives, and complements to noun phrases in the main clause (see the table).

Subject	That she can do these tricks seems unbelievable. **Subj**
DO	Ben knew (that) his brother stole money from their parents. **DO**
PredN	The truth is (that) no one wants to claim responsibility for this gaffe. **PredN**
Comp to Adj	It is natural (that) people appreciate life more when they are older. **Comp to Adj "natural"**
Comp to NP	Fans still can't digest the fact (that) Chris Brown attacked Rihanna. **Comp to NP "the fact"**

- The COMP "that" is put in brackets in all sentences except the first one. This is because it **cannot** be deleted when the Noun Clause functions as the Subject, but it can be deleted elsewhere.

- Here is a diagram of the second sentence from the table. It shows that the COMP "that" does **not** become a constituent of the subordinate clause. The noun clause has its own Subject "his brother," VT "stole," DO "money," and PP:Adv of source "from their parents."

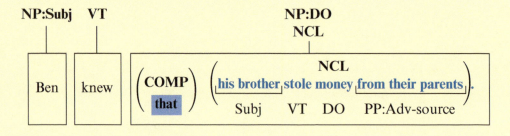

Things You Need to Know About

Subordinate Clauses

Quick Quiz 1: Which "that"?

Determine the function of the word "that" in the following sentences:

(1)   **That** car is not mine.   _____

(2)   **That** was an amazing experience.   _____

(3)   I've never seen a place **that** beautiful.   _____

(4)   The man **that** I talked to is my dad.   _____

(5)   I know **that** he is tired.   _____

(6)   **That** movie is boring.   _____

(7)   He is always late. **That** is irresponsible.   _____

(8)   Movies **that** make the most money at the box office usually are not
      low-budget psychological dramas.   _____

(9)   I know **that** my parents always support me.   _____

(10) **That** my parents always support me helps me in everything I do.   _____

Things You Need to Know About

Subordinate Clauses

- Students sometimes have trouble distinguishing between Noun Clauses and Relative Clauses. The following table will help you keep them apart.

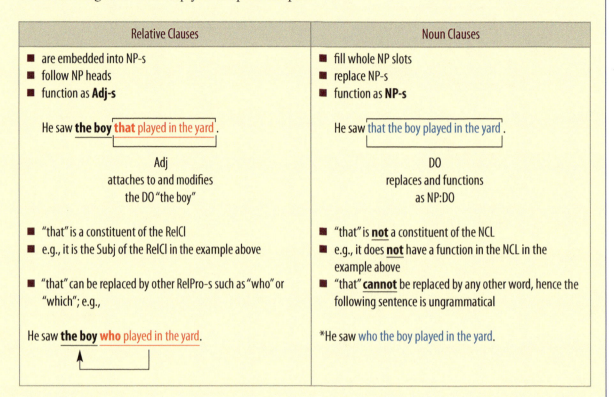

Relative Clauses	Noun Clauses
■ are embedded into NP-s ■ follow NP heads ■ function as **Adj-s** He saw **the boy that** played in the yard. Adj attaches to and modifies the DO "the boy" ■ "that" is a constituent of the RelCl ■ e.g., it is the Subj of the RelCl in the example above ■ "that" can be replaced by other RelPro-s such as "who" or "which"; e.g., He saw **the boy who** played in the yard.	■ fill whole NP slots ■ replace NP-s ■ function as **NP-s** He saw that the boy played in the yard. DO replaces and functions as NP:DO ■ "that" is **not** a constituent of the NCL ■ e.g., it does **not** have a function in the NCL in the example above ■ "that" **cannot** be replaced by any other word, hence the following sentence is ungrammatical *He saw who the boy played in the yard.

- Wh-clauses are also noun clauses;

  They are introduced by a Wh-word: who, when, where, how, how often, why, etc.

- Unlike the COMP "that," Wh-subordinators (Wh-Sub) are constituents in the Wh-Clause, and can have various functions; e.g., Subj, DO, IO, Adv, Det, etc.

Things You Need to Know About

Subordinate Clauses

■ NCLs in general, and wh-clauses in particular have the same functions as nouns or other nominals (adapted from Rodby and Winterowd, 2005).

Subject	Noun:	Magic baffles people.
	NCL:	What she can do baffles people.
DO	Noun:	Shoppers seek bargains.
	NCL:	Shoppers seek whatever costs least.
IO	Noun:	Police give speeders citations.
	NCL:	Police give whoever exceeds the speed limit citations.
Obj/Prep	Noun:	The children laughed at the clown.
	NCL:	The children laughed at what the clown did.
PredN	Noun:	The problem is money.
	NCL:	The problem is how much this project will cost.
OC	Noun:	The boss called Jack a hypocrite.
	NCL:	The boss called Jack whatever popped into his mind.
Appositive NP	Noun:	His home, the whole three-storey house, collapsed.
	NCL:	His home, what was left of it after the earthquake, collapsed.
Vocative	Noun:	Father, please rescue the dog from these people.
	NCL:	Whoever has the power, please rescue the dog from these people.

■   The diagrams below show that Wh-Subs are constituents of their respective clauses:

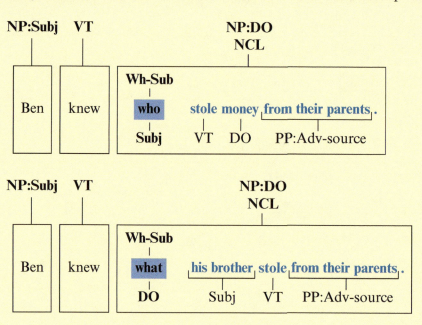

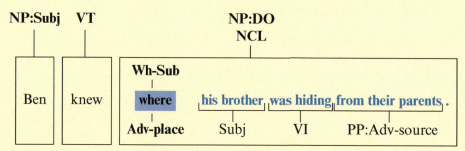

Quick Quiz 2

I. What is the function of the Wh-clause (in blue colour) in the sentence?
II. What is the function of the underlined Wh-word within the Wh-clause?

		Wh-Clause	Wh-Sub
(1)	The philanthropist gave <u>whoever</u> was needy financial help.	_____	_____
(2)	<u>What</u> I like about our library is that it is close to my building.	_____	_____
(3)	Father forgot <u>who</u> had set the garage on fire.	_____	_____
(4)	Do you know to <u>whom</u> Lily gave the note?	_____	_____
(5)	She arrived at <u>what</u> looked like a small village.	_____	_____

Things You Need to Know About
Subordinate Clauses

- **Whether/if** are different from Wh-Subs.

- They do not function as nouns or adverbs within their clauses.

- They are simply Subord.

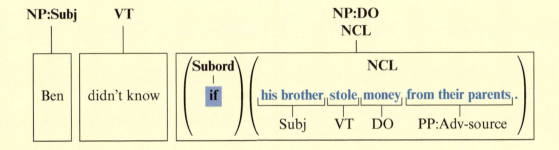

Adverbial Clauses

- Adverbial clauses can be for time, cause, condition, manner, purpose, etc.;
- They are introduced by Subordinating Conjunctions such as if, before, after, as soon as, when, although, etc. (see sentences (1)-(6) below);
- Adverbial clauses (in red colour) can occur before or after the main clause (in green colour); compare sentences (4) and (5):

   (1) If we get paid today, I'm going to buy this nice pair of shoes.
   (2) After we get paid today, I'm going to buy this nice pair of shoes.
   (3) As soon as we get paid today, I'm going to buy this nice pair of shoes.
   (4) Before we get paid today, I can't buy this nice pair of shoes.
   (5) I can't buy this nice pair of shoes before we get paid today.
   (6) Although we get paid today, I still won't be able to buy this nice pair of shoes.

- Note that words like *after, before, as, like,* etc. can introduce AdvCl-s, and hence function as Subord, or they can be used with NPs to form PPs, hence they function as prepositions.

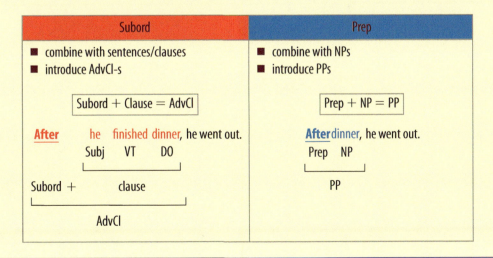

Exercises

A. Choose one of the following labels that best describes the grammatical role of the underlined word or group of words **in either the main clause or the relative clause**:

Subj, DO, IO, OC, Obj/Prep, PredN, RelCl, RelDet, or None .

1. They shouldn't be selling paper coffee cups **which** have plastic lids since the plastic lids are non-recyclable. [from radio clip "Problems with Coffee cups," cbc.ca]

   _____

2. The letter was signed by **the people who were trying to acquire the company**.

   _____

3. Her husband wanted her to put on the dress **he bought her for their first wedding anniversary**.

   _____

4. Her husband wanted her to put on the dress he bought **her** for their first wedding anniversary.

   _____

5. Her husband wanted her to put on **the dress he bought her for their first wedding anniversary**.

   _____

6. The numerous rejections of my scripts **I had to deal with as a university student** just made me a better writer.

   _____

7. He became **a man who knew no fear**.

   _____

8. In case of emergency, follow **the instructions the building manager gave you**.

   _____

9. In case of emergency, follow the instructions **the building manager** gave you.

   _____

10. Applicants **whose** photos do not comply with the requirements will be asked to resubmit their applications.

_____

11. **Applicants** whose photos do not comply with the requirements will be asked to resubmit their applications.

_____

12. J. K. Rowling finally created in her "Harry Potter" series the fantastic and adventurous world **she had been dreaming of**.
[Harry Potter Series, thebest100lists.com]

_____

13. I found January Jones' dress for the 2010 Emmys **a bold and smart choice which revealed her personality and wit**.

_____

14. The children **who** he went to choir with made fun of his unusual voice.

_____

15. Russians find the last book **Tolstoy wrote** the most accurate reflection of life in Russia at the time.

_____

16. Russians find **the last book** Tolstoy wrote the most accurate reflection of life in Russia at the time.

_____

17. Russians find the last book Tolstoy wrote **the most accurate reflection of life in Russia at the time**.

_____

B. Count how many of the requested items the sentence contains. In your answer, provide the total number of items; e.g., zero/none, one, two, three, etc. (item/s).

1. Readers who enjoy political fables embrace the dark vision of the future George Orwell paints in his book "1984."
   [adapted from 1984 Orwell Book Summary, ghanadiscuss.com]

   *How many **relative clauses** are there in sentence 1?*

   _____

2. Who knows the truth about the queen's lost treasure?

   *How many **relative clauses** are there in sentence 2?*

   _____

3. Each student who attended the reading made a list of books that had influenced them and whose writer they wanted to meet in person.

   *How many **relative pronouns and/or relative determiners** are there in sentence 3?*

   _____

4. A Tsar is a ruler in Medieval Europe who claims the same rank as a Roman emperor.
   [from Tsar, wikipedia.org]

   *How many **subjects** are there in sentence 4?*

   _____

5. A Tsar is a ruler in Medieval Europe who claims the same rank as a Roman emperor.
   [from Tsar, wikipedia.org]

   *How many **direct objects** are there in sentence 5?*

   _____

6. a) As a technical writer, I often edited documents in **which** people used the wrong word. [from quickanddirtytips.com]

   b) A suitcase **which** has lost its handle is useless. [from "Restrictive . . .", proz.com]

   c) **Which** one of these do I need to use?

   d) **Which** people do you think are happier—the uneducated or the most educated among us?

   e) Think of the comparative ease with **which** we say "I'm sorry!"

*How many of the underlined "wh"-words in sentences 6a to 6e are **relative pronouns**?*

---

7. a) Change sounds good; I've been thinking about **that** for a while.

   b) I don't know why **that** lady keeps bothering me.

   c) Can you think of anything else **that** still has to be done?

   d) If you ask me, the show is overrated and not **that** interesting.

   e) The tree **that** was knocked down by the recent storm was over one hundred years old.

*How many of the underlined instances of "that" in sentences 7a to 7e are **relative pronouns**?*

C. Identify the requested structure, if any, by underlining or copying it.

   1. *The Subject of the main clause*
   The man who was saved by the night patrol last night is from Mexico.

   2. *The Logical and the Grammatical Subject of the relative clause*
   The man who was saved by the night patrol last night is from Mexico.

   3. *The Obj/Prep*
   She was obviously talking about someone who she had never met before.

   4. *The DO*
   Liam hated the restaurant where his friends wanted to meet every Wednesday.

   5. *The RelCl*
   The crowd applauded the athletes who competed so vigorously for the country they loved so much.

D. Choose one of the following labels that best describes the grammatical role of the underlined word or group of words **in either the main clause or the subordinate clause**:

AdvCl: Adv	NCL: Obj/Prep
NCL: Comp to Adj	NCL: PredN
NCL: Comp to NP	NCL: Subj
NCL: OC	None
NCL: DO	RelCl:Adj

1. SFU's efforts make us confident **that energy self-sufficiency by 2016 is fully realizable**. [from the SFU website, sfu.ca]

   _____

2. People reported being happiest **when engaged in what they were doing versus allowing their minds to wander**. [from "Daydreaming . . . ," scientificamerican.com]

   _____

3. People reported being happiest when engaged in **what they were doing** versus allowing their minds to wander. [from "Daydreaming . . . ," scientificamerican.com]

   _____

4. Psychologists at Harvard found out **people spend nearly half their waking hours thinking about something other than what they're doing**. [from "Daydreaming . . . ," scientificamerican.com]

   _____

5. SFU "has not only consistently met its rigorous energy-saving targets, but has raised the bar for **what Power Smart excellence truly is**," says BC Hydro president and CEO, Dave Cobb. [from the SFU website, sfu.ca]

   _____

6. **Where people like to go on a vacation** can tell you a lot about their character.

   _____

E. What is the function of the underlined word in the subordinate clause in which it occurs? Choose one label from the following list:

Adv	Obj/Prep
Adj	PredAdj
DO	PredAdv
IO	PredN
None	Subj
OC	

1. SFU "has not only consistently met its rigorous energy-saving targets, but has raised the bar for **what** Power Smart excellence truly is," says BC Hydro president and CEO, Dave Cobb. [from the SFU website, sfu.ca]

   _____

2. **Where** people like to go on a vacation can tell you a lot about their character.

   _____

3. People reported being happiest when engaged in **what** they were doing versus allowing their minds to wander. [from "Daydreaming . . .", scientificamerican.com]

   _____

4. SFU's efforts make us confident **that** energy self-sufficiency by 2016 is fully realizable. [from the SFU website, sfu.ca]

   _____

5. Take a moment to remember **who** the seats in our Priority Area are reserved for. [sign on a bus]

   _____

Answers to Quick Quiz 1

1. DemonD
2. DemonPro
3. Qual
4. RelPro
5. COMP *(in NCL:DO; note that the COMP can be deleted)*
6. DemonD
7. DemonPro
8. RelPro
9. COMP *(in NCL:DO; note that the COMP can be deleted)*
10. COMP *(in NCL:Subj; note that the COMP **cannot** be deleted; note also that the sentence contains a RelCl "I do" with a deleted RelPro "that which")*

Answers to Quick Quiz 2

	Wh-Clause	Wh-Sub
1.	IO	Subj
2.	Subj	DO
3.	DO	Subj
4.	DO	Obj/Prep or IO
5.	Obj/Prep	Subj

Answers to Exercises

A.
1. Subj   (of the RelCl)
2. Obj/Prep   (Prep "by")
3. RelCl   (deleted RelPro)
4. IO   (of the verb "bought" in the RelCl)
5. DO
6. RelCl   (deleted RelPro)
7. PredN
8. DO
9. Subj   (of the RelCl with deleted RelPro)
10. RelDet   (of the RelCl with deleted RelPro)
11. None   (part of the Subj, not the whole one)
12. RelCl   (deleted RelPro)
13. OC
14. Obj/Prep   (Prep "with" in the RelCl)
15. RelCl   (deleted RelPro)
16. None   (part of the DO "the last book Tolstoy wrote")
17. OC   (of the Vc "find")

B. 1. Two   ("who enjoy political fables" and
                         "G. Orwell paints in his book '1984'")
  2. None   ("who" is an InterPro in a question)
  3. Three   ("who," "that," and "whose")
  4. Two   ("a Tsar" and "who")
  5. One   ("the same rank as a Roman emperor")
  6. Three   (a), (b), and (e)
  7. Two   (c) and (e)

C. 1. The man who was saved by the night patrol last night is from Mexico.

                        Subj of the main clause

  2. The man who was saved by the night patrol last night is from Mexico.

           Gram. Subj   Logical Subj
           of the RelCl   of the RelCl

  3. She was obviously talking about someone who she had never met before.

                             Obj/Prep "about"

  4. Liam hated the restaurant where his friends wanted to meet every Wednesday.

                      DO of the main clause

  5. The crowd applauded the athletes who competed so vigorously for the country they loved so much.

                                                            RelCl1

                                         RelCl2

D. 1. NCL:Comp to Adj
  2. AdvCl:Adv
  3. NCL:Obj/Prep   (Prep "in")
  4. NCL:DO   (of "found out"; deleted COMP)
  5. NCL:Obj/Prep   (Prep "for")
  6. NCL:Subj

E. 1. PredN
  2. Adv   (of place)
  3. DO
  4. None   (COMP; doesn't have a function in the Subordinate Clause)
  5. Obj/Prep   (Prep "for")

Non-Finite Verbals

Non-finite verbal phrases, or non-finite verbals, are verb-like units that do not function as the MV of a sentence. They do not have tense, though they may have aspect. They can occur in both the active and the passive voices.

Jack is imagining the future.	MV = is imagining
The man **imagining the future** is Jack.	MV = is
Imagining the future, Jack wasted the whole afternoon.	MV = wasted
Imagining the future is a waste of time.	MV = is
To imagine the future is a waste of time.	MV = is

I. Participles

Participles and participial phrases tend to function as adjectival modifiers that are closely connected with an NP.

The woman **writing the novel** is Jane.
Tony is the guy **fixing the sink**.
The tree **damaged by the wind** is in the back yard.

Aspect and voice of participles

The simple active and simple passive participles are the most common types. However, more complex types sometimes occur, particularly in written English. Note that the participle (present or past) is always named according to the form of the first word of the non-finite verbal. In the examples below, the underlined portion is the participle itself; the italicized portion is the full participial phrase.

simple active present participle	The woman *__writing__ the novel* is Jane.
perfective, active present participle	*__Having written__ twelve pages,* Jane stopped working.
perfective, progressive, active present participle	*__Having been writing__ for ten years,* Jane was very experienced.
simple passive present participle	The book *__being written__ by Jane* is a suspense novel.
perfective, passive present participle	*__Having been written__ over thirty years ago,* the computer manual was outdated.
past participle	The novel *__written__ by Jane* is delightful.

II. Gerunds

Gerunds function as nouns and, within the sentence, gerund phrases behave as NPs. In the examples below, the underlined portion is the gerund itself; the italicized portion is the full gerund phrase. Each italicized unit is also an NP.

__Kayaking__ is a very enjoyable sport.
Marilyn prefers *__swimming__ with her friends.*
Grace thanked him by *__offering__ him dinner.*

Quickly __finishing__ his work is Fred's specialty.
Ted's __leaving__ the company surprised us.
My __leaving__ the company surprised them.

Aspect and voice of gerunds

simple active gerund	She regrets **sleeping** *all day.*
perfective active gerund	She regrets **having slept** *all day.*
perfective progressive active gerund	She regrets **having been sleeping** (when you called).
simple passive gerund	The cat hates **being bathed**.
perfective passive gerund	The cat hates **having been bathed.**

III. Infinitives

Infinitives and the phrases they belong to can play a variety of roles within the sentence. In the examples below, the underlined portion is the infinitive itself; the italicized portion is the full infinitive phrase.

Infinitive NPs

__To err__ is human.
Keiko prefers *__to stay__* *at home.*
Jack's goal is *__to complete__* *the work before Tuesday.*

Aspect and voice of infinitives

(simple active)	Chauncey loves *__to watch__* *television.*
(perfective active)	By the time I'm sixty, I intend *__to have travelled__* *around the world.*
(progressive active)	He likes *__to be working__* *in his garden.*
(perfective progressive active)	*__To have been living__* *in Provence for a year* must have been wonderful.
(simple passive)	Move to Nebraska? I'd prefer *__to be eaten__* *by sharks!*
(perfective passive)	I would like *__to have been introduced__* *to your friend.*

Quick Quiz

Complete the following checklist, indicating which verbs can take a gerund object, which can take an infinitive object, and which can take both. Note any problems that arise in your classification.

	Gerund	Infinitive	Both
begin			
mind			
expect			
refuse			
endeavor			
stop			
remember			
intend			
can't bear			
dislike			

Additional examples of infinitive constructions

She took Broad Street ***to avoid*** *the heavy traffic.*
She took Broad Street ***in order to*** *avoid the heavy traffic.*

John is eager ***to leave****.*
The waterfall is wonderful ***to see****.*

To visit *Peru* is Carol's fondest wish.
It is Carol's fondest wish ***to visit*** *Peru.*

To see *the waterfall at night* is marvelous.
It is marvelous ***to see*** *the waterfall at night.*

It is unusual for Fido ***to ignore*** *his dinner.*

Things You Need to Know About
Non-finite Verbals

Participle Phrases

- Participial Phrases contain non-tensed verb forms;

- They are two types:
  - present participial phrases (PresPartPh), and
  - past participial phrases (PastPartPh);

- They can be derived from relative clauses by deleting the RelPro:Subj and Aux-BE, as shown below:

> RELCL
>
> The children who were bullying him in elementary school were spoiled kids of wealthy parents.
>
> | Delete Subj.Pro and Aux-BE |
>
> The children ~~who were~~ bullying him in elementary school were spoiled kids of wealthy parents.
>
> Present participial phrases
>
> The children bullying him in elementary school were spoiled kids of wealthy parents.

> RELCL
>
> Some of the treats which were made the previous day were stale by the day of the party.
>
> | Delete Subj.Pro and Aux-BE |
>
> Some of the treats ~~which were~~ made the previous day were stale by the day of the party.
>
> Past Participial Phrase
>
> Some of the treats made the previous day were stale by the day of the party.

- Just like RelCls, the participial phrases in these examples function as adjectives: "bullying him in elementary school" is a PresPartPh:Adj, modifying the NP "the children," while "made the previous day" is a PastPartPh:Adj, modifying the NP "some of the treats";

- Verbs which cannot be made progressive, have to be made into present participles (in addition to deleting Aux-BE and the RelPro) to derive a PresPartPh; e.g.,

> RelCl
> having
> The students ~~who have~~ the best handwriting tend to get higher marks.
>
> PresPartPh
> The students having the best handwriting tend to get higher marks.

Things You Need to Know About

Non-finite Verbals

- PastPartPh-s are always derived from passive clauses; e.g.,

    They made the treats the previous day.   [original active clause]

    The treats were made the previous day (by them).   [passive]

- In PastPartPh, the verb may be followed by a PP functioning as an **Adv. of agency**, or the agent phrase may be deleted; e.g.,

    a play created in the early thirties **(by an unknown writer)**

- The verbs of PastPartPh-s are always transitive: VT, Vg, or Vc.

Infinitive Phrases

- Infinitive Phrases (InfPh) contain non-tensed verb forms;

- Infinitive Phrases have two functions:
    - as NPs,
    - as Adverbs.

- Here are some examples of InfPh-s functioning as NPs and as Adv-s:

Subject	To swim in the ocean is a great pleasure. **Subj** Note that "to" is not a preposition when a Verb follows; it's an infinitive marker.
DO	I decided to read that novel immediately. **DO**
PredN	His job is to cook dinner. **PredN** My goal remains to graduate in December. **PredN**
OC	She helped me find a great gift for my mom's birthday. **OC of the Vc "helped"**
Comp to Adj	It is natural for students to be nervous before exams. **Comp to Adj "natural"**
Comp to NP	I didn't like the proposal to meet on Sundays. **Comp to NP "the proposal"**

Things You Need to Know About

Non-finite Verbals

Adverb	He let the blinds down⌐to get some rest⌐. **InfPh:Adv-reason** = ***in order to*** *get some rest* *Answers the question "Why? For what reason?"* *They stopped by*⌐*to say "hi."*⌐ **InfPh:Adv-reason**

- Infinitives are usually introduced by the infinitive marker "to";

- Some verbs like "let," "make," "have," and "bid" require infinitives without the infinitive marker "to"; the verb "help" can be followed by infinitives with or without "to"; e.g.,

  The teachers **didn't let** us ___ use dictionaries.
  She **helped** me (to) find a great gift for my mom's birthday.
  You **can't make** me ___ do it.

- It is also possible to have infinitives with their own subject, in which case the infinitives are introduced by two infinitive markers: "for" and "to," and the subject of the infinitive is placed between the two markers; e.g.,

  It is natural **for** students **to** be nervous before exams.

  Here, "students" is the subject of the "for . . . to"-infinitive.

- Infinitive Phrases can be analyzed as reduced NCL-s; e.g.,

           to
  He told us ~~that we should~~ be there on time.
          NCL

  He told us to be there on time.
          InfP:DO

           to
  It is natural ~~that people~~ get nervous before exams.
          NCL: Comp to Adj "natural"

  It is natural to get nervous before exams.
          InfPh: Comp to Adj

  It is natural **for** people **to** get nervous before exams.
          InfPh: Comp to Adj (for . . . to Inf)

Things You Need to Know About

Non-finite Verbals

- However, it is not always possible to choose between an InfPh and a NCL, because many structures allow one or the other, or neither; e.g.,

      I believe that we are on time.
      *I believe to be on time.
              The VT "believe" requires a That-Cl, and does not allow an InfPh;

  *She wants that she goes on a vacation.
  She **wants to** go on a vacation.
          The Caten "want to" must be followed by an infinitive verb (not InfPh); it doesn't allow a That-Cl

Gerund Phrases

- Gerund Phrases (GerPh) contain non-tensed verb forms;
- Gerund Phrases always function as NPs; below are examples of the NP functions they may have:

Subject	Swimming in the river is dangerous. **Subj**
DO	I enjoy reading detective stories. **DO of "enjoy"**
PredN	His job is cooking delicious meals for the family. **PredN**
Obj/Prep	We are thinking about travelling to Spain. **Obj/Prep "about"**

- The "**-ing**" ending of gerunds; e.g., swimm**ing**, marks gerunds just like the infinitive marker "to" marks InfPh; both markers can be thought of as Subord;

- GerPh could be compound; in the following example, three compound GerPh-s function as the object of the preposition "about":

  They were thinking about selling their house, moving to another city, and starting a new life.

                  Cpd GerPh-s: Obj/Prep "about"

- Some gerunds have their own subjects;

- Such GerPh-s are called Gerunds with Genitives; in the following example "his mom's" is the Subj of the gerund "meddling," and the whole GerPh is the DO of VT "didn't like":

  He didn't like his mom's meddling into his life.

          GerPh:DO

Things You Need to Know About
Non-finite Verbals

- Sometimes, it is difficult for students to distinguish between PresPartPh and GerPh because of the superficial similarity in the form; i.e., the non-finite verbs in both phrases end in "-ing";
- The following table will help you keep them apart:

Present Participle Phrases	Gerund Phrases
Present participial phrases are derived from underlying structures with BE &"-ing"; e.g.,	Gerunds are **not** derived this way; e.g.,
Underlying RelCl:Adj **i.a.** The mayor spoke with **the people** ~~who are~~ **fighting drug addiction.** **i.b.** The mayor spoke with **the people fighting drug addiction.** *PresPartPh:Adj*	**ii.** The mayor said (that) **fighting drug addiction** requires money. *GerPh:Subj of the NCL* *"(that) fighting drug addiction requires money"*
PresPartPhs **never fill noun slots**; they **function as Adj-s or Adv-s.**	GerPh-s **always fill noun slots.**

- Finally, compare these three sentences, and decide in which sentences the underlined set of words forms a constituent:

  (1) The man **skating on the rink** is my dad.
  (2) The man is **skating on the rink**.
  (3) The man loves **skating on the rink**.

- In (1):

  - "skating on the rink" is similar to "the skating man" (Adj),
  - answers the question "Which man?" and
  - can be viewed as derived from a RelCl:Adj "the man who is skating on the rink";

- therefore, it is a **PresPartPh:Adj.**

- In (2):

  - "skating" is the PresPart form of the verb, and it is a part of the MV "is skating";
  - "is" is the AUX BE, which combines with the PresPart form to make the present progressive tense-aspect combination;
  - it answers the question "What is the man doing?," while "on the rink" is a PP:Adv-place, and answers the question "Where?";

- therefore, the underlined set of words is **not a constituent.**

Things You Need to Know About

Non-finite Verbals

- In (3):

  - "skating on the rink" is the DO of the VT "love";
  - it has an NP function similar to "sports" in "The man loves sports," or to "the rink" in "The man loves the rink";

- therefore, it is **a GerPh:DO.**

Exercises

A. **a)** Parse each sentence.

b) Bracket all the participial, gerund, and infinitive phrases.

c) For participial phrases (and participles that stand alone as modifiers), identify the noun modified (i.e., the logical subject of the participle).

d) Indicate the role in the sentence played by all gerund phrases and infinitive phrases. (NP: Subj, NP: DO, NP: ObjPrep, Adv, Comp to Adj, Comp to NP, etc.)

1. Watering the plants daily is his responsibility.

_____

2. Rebecca plans to run three miles before heading to work.

_____

3. He's returning to the hotel early to get ready for an exciting evening.

_____

4. Purring loudly, the kitten jumped into my lap.

_____

5. In an effort to reduce crime on the downtown east side, the city is sending out more police officers.

_____

6. With all that RAM, I can have many programs run simultaneously on my laptop.

_____

7. A lot of energy is needed for running a marathon.

_____

8. Alan will find practicing Zen a valuable experience.

_____

9. Last night the neighbour's dog's barking disturbed my sleep.

_____

10. An injection is now available to prevent the flu that's going around.

_____

11. She has a term paper to write by next week.

_____

12. He annoys me with his constant complaining about everything going on in the neighbourhood.

_____

13. Dee wants to learn to write romance novels.

_____

14. Zoe likes to do cryptic crossword puzzles to keep her mind active.

_____

15. When I saw the damaged window, I began to suspect that something was wrong.

_____

16. They do the community a service by working in the soup kitchen.

_____

17. I don't intend to drink coffee after eight.

_____

18. To have loved and lost is sad.

_____

19. However, it is sadder not to have loved at all.

_____

20. On hearing about his promotion, Ken's first impulse was to open a bottle of Champagne.

_____

21. It's easy for him to get to work on the bus.

_____

22. Flying planes can be dangerous.

_____

23. It's unusual to see traffic on our street.

_____

24. She left during the night.

_____

25. Ned abhors vacuuming.

_____

B. Choose one of the following labels that best describes the grammatical role of the underlined word or group of words **in either the main clause or the subordinate clause**:

GerPh:DO	InfPh:Adv
GerPh:Obj/Prep	InfPh:Comp to Adj
GerPh:PredN	InfPh:Comp to NP
GerPh:Subj	InfPh:OC
PresPartPh:Adj	InfPh:DO
Past PartPh:Adj	InfPh:PredN
None	InfPh:Subj

1. People reported **being happiest when engaged in what they were doing versus allowing their minds to wander**.
[from "Daydreaming . . . ," scientificamerican.com]

_____

2. People reported being happiest when engaged in what they were doing versus allowing their minds **to wander**.
[from "Daydreaming . . . ," scientificamerican.com]

_____

3. Often **sitting back and letting your thoughts drift** may be one of the most pleasant things. [from "Daydreaming . . . ," scientificamerican.com]

_____

4. Often sitting back and letting your thoughts **drift** may be one of the most pleasant things. [from "Daydreaming . . . ," scientificamerican.com]

_____

5. Britain's queen has launched a series of official pages **offering the website's 500 million users daily updates on her engagements**, the royal household said on Sunday. [from "British Queen Joins . . . ," nationnews.com]

_____

6. Twenty-seven percent of employers think many workers are **giving phony excuses because of all the stress and burnout caused by the recession and its aftermath**. [from "The Year's Most Ridiculous Excuses . . . ," forbes.com]

_____

7. Twenty-seven percent of employers think many workers are giving phony excuses because of all the stress and burnout **caused by the recession and its aftermath**. [from "The Year's Most Ridiculous Excuses . . . ," forbes.com]

_____

8. Humans, to a degree unmatched by other animals, are capable of **thinking about things outside the here and now**. [from "Daydreaming . . . ," scientificamerican.com]

_____

9. In an October 22 ruling, the B.C. Labour Relations Board said West Coast Mazda had proper cause **to fire the two employees for making "disrespectful, damaging, and derogatory comments on Facebook."** [from "First Clear Facebook Firing . . . ," globaltvbc.com]

_____

10. In an October 22 ruling, the B.C. Labour Relations Board said West Coast Mazda had proper cause to fire the two employees for **making "disrespectful, damaging, and derogatory comments on Facebook."** [from "First Clear Facebook Firing . . . ," globaltvbc.com]

_____

11. SFU was the first major Canadian university **to install a female president—Pauline Jewett in 1974**; she was a former university professor and a member of Parliament.
[from the SFU website, sfu.ca]

_____

12. SFU was the first Canadian university to establish a forensic laboratory in 1999 that uses entomology—the study of bugs—**to help solve murders nationally and internationally**.
[from the SFU website, sfu.ca]

_____

Answers to Selected Exercises

B. **1.** GerPh:DO

    2. InfPh:OC   (of Vc "allow")

    3. GerPh:Subj

    4. InfPh:OC   (of Vc "let")

    5. PresPartPh:Adj   (modifying "a series of official pages")

    6. None   ("are giving": MV; "giving": PresPart forms of the verb, but not a PresPartPh)

    7. PastPartPh:Adj   (modifying "all the stress and burnout")

    8. GerPh:Obj/Prep   (Prep "of")

    9. InfPh:Comp to NP   (DO: "proper cause")

   10. GerPh:Obj/Prep   (Prep "for")

   11. InfPh:Comp to NP   (PredN: "the first major Canadian University . . . 1974")

   12. InfPh:Adv   ("in order to help . . .")

The Secret Life of Non-Finite Verbals

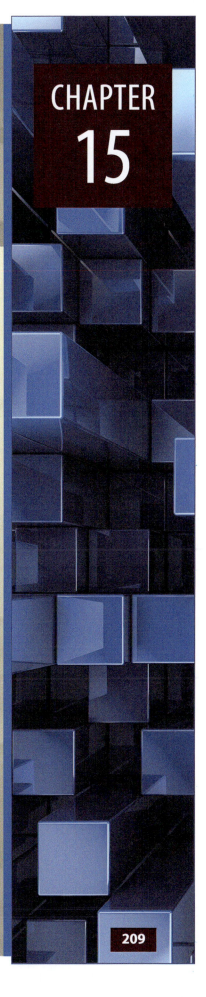

When you are parsing sentences containing a gerund, infinitive, or participle, you should use the labels Ger, Inf, PresPart, and PastPart. The sentence below contains a gerund:

PropN	VT	Ger	Prep	DefArt	N
Gene	enjoys	singing	in	the	rain.

However, it is important to recognize that non-finite verbal phrases have internal structure and logic. The preceding example contains a gerund phrase ("singing in the rain") that functions as a DO and that has the following components:

Gene = the logical subject of the gerund
singing = Ger (VI)
in the rain = PP (adverbial modifier)

To provide a thorough analysis, include the verbal type in parentheses as in the parsing below:

PropN	VT	Ger (VI)	Prep	DefArt	N
Gene	enjoys	singing	in	the	rain.

Additional examples:

PropN	VT	Ger (VT)	PossProD	N	Prep	DefArt	N
Debbie	likes	walking	her	dog	in	the	rain.

The gerund phrase (walking her dog in the rain) plays the role of DO in the sentence.

Debbie = the logical subject of the gerund
walking = Ger (VT)
her dog = NP:DO of the gerund
in the rain = PP (adverbial modifier)

```
DefArt  N    VT     Inf (BE)  Adj
The     cat  hates  to be     uncomfortable.
```

The infinitive phrase (to be uncomfortable) plays the role of DO in the sentence.

The cat = the logical subject of the infinitive
to be = Inf (BE)
uncomfortable = PredAdj within the infinitive phrase

Things You Need to Know About

The Secret Life of Non-finite Verbals

Participial Phrases

- Let's look in more detail into the internal structure of Participial Phrases:

Past Participial Phrase

(1) Some of the treats made the previous day were stale by the day of the party.

some of the treats: NP head of Subj
made the previous day: PastPartPh:Adj (modifying "some of the treats")
    made: PastPart (VT)   [passive, comes from "someone made the treats"]
    the previous day: NP:Adv-time   [contains: DefArt Adj N]

Present Participial Phrase

(2) The children bullying him in elementary school were spoiled kids of wealthy parents.

the children: NP head of the Subj
bullying him in elementary school: PresPartPh:Adj (modifying "the children")
    bullying: PresPart (VT)
    him: DO of "bullying"
    in elementary school: PP:Adv-place   [contains: Prep Adj N]

Infinitive Phrases

- Let's look in more detail into the internal structure of Infinitive Phrases:

(3) The board's decision was to close our department.

- To close our department: InfPh:PredN of BE
  - to close: Inf (VT)
  - our department: DO of VT "close"

(4) She helped me find a great gift for my mom.

- find a great gift for my mom: InfPh:OC of Vc "helped"
  (Note that "me" is the DO of Vc "helped")
  - find: Inf (Vg) ["find a gift for my mom" or "find my mom a great gift"]
  - a great gift: DO of Vg "find"   [contains IndefArt Adj N]
  - my mom: IO of Vg "find"   [contains PossProD N]

(5) She helped me find a great gift for my mom's birthday.

- find a great gift for my mom's birthday: InfPh:OC of Vc "helped"
  (Note that "me" is the DO of Vc "helped")
  - find: Inf (VT)   ["find something"]
  - a great gift for mom's birthday: DO of VT "find"
    - a great gift: NP head of the DO   [contains IndefArt Adj N]
    - for my mom's birthday: PP:Adj (modifying "a great gift"; answers the question "What kind of gift?");   [contains Prep PossProD GenN N]

Things You Need to Know About

The Secret Life of Non-finite Verbals

Inf—head of InfPh or MV?

- It is sometimes hard to decide whether an infinitive is the head of an InfPh that fills a NP slot, or head of the MV constituent; compare (1) and (2) below:

(1) She asked to see the principal.
             ask (VT): MV
             to see the principal: InfPh:DO of "ask"
                  to see (VT): head of InfPh
                  the principal: DO of the Inf

(2) He had to see the principal.
           had to see: MV
                had to: Caten
                see (VT): head of the MV
         the principal: DO of "see"

- Therefore, (1) contain an InfPh, but (2), although it contains an infinitive verb ("see"), does not contain an InfPh.

Extraposed InfPh-s and InfPh with Subjects

- InfPh-s are often extraposed in structures, where the expletive "it" is the Grammatical subject, and the InfPh is the Logical Subject; below is an example with a "for . . . to" infinitive:

    For Myra to admit she's made such a silly mistake is difficult.

InfPh:Subj

    It is difficult for Myra to admit she's made such a silly mistake.

Gram.Subj;   Extraposed InfPh: **Log.Subj** &
                                  Comp to Adj "difficult"

- "For" and "to" function as a single infinitive marker, similar to Subord

- As we mentioned in Chapter 14, the NP between "for" and "to" is the Subject of the InfPh

- In the last sentence, repeated below, "for Myra to admit" is the 4-word Inf (VT)—head of the InfPh "for Myra to admit she's made such a silly mistake," and "Myra" is the subject of the Inf; note also that the InfPh contains a NCL (That-Cl): "she's made such a silly mistake."

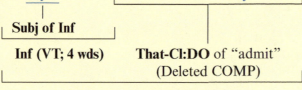

    It is difficult for **Myra** to admit she's made such a silly mistake.

                      Subj of Inf

              Inf (VT; 4 wds)   **That-Cl:DO** of "admit"
                                       (Deleted COMP)

              InfPh:Comp to Adj "difficult"

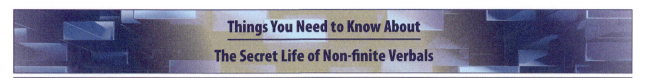

Things You Need to Know About

The Secret Life of Non-finite Verbals

Gerund Phrases

■ Let's look in more detail into the internal structure of Gerund Phrases:

> I enjoy reading detective stories.
>> reading detective stories: GerPh: DO of "enjoy"
>>> reading: Ger (VT)
>>> detective stories: DO of Ger "reading"   [contains N:Adj N]

GerPh with Subjects

■ We also noted in Chapter 14 that Gerunds can have subjects; for example, in the PossProD "his" and the Gen "mom's" together make up the Subj of the Ger "meddling"; "meddling" is the head of the GerPh "his mom's meddling into his life":

> He didn't like **his mom's meddling into his life** .

|Subj of Ger Ger (VI)   PP:Adv|

GerPh:DO

> his mom's meddling into his life: GerPh:DO of "didn't like"
>> his mom's: Subj of the Ger   [contains PossProD GenN]
>> meddling: Ger (VI)
>> into his life: PP:Adv-place   [contains Prep PossProD N]

Exercises

A. Determine the status of the underlined words in the sentences below. For verbs, use the labels VI, VT, etc. For participles, use PresPart(type) or PastPart(type). For preposed participles, use Adj For gerunds, use Ger(type).

1. **Making** money is the only thing that interests him.

   _____

2. You should let **sleeping** dogs lie.

   _____

3. Speak loudly so the people **sitting** in the back can hear you.

   _____

4. You can press your shirt on this **ironing** board.

   _____

5. A great deal of the information **posted** on *Wikipedia* is false.

   _____

6. Was the big pot **simmering** on the stove?

   _____

7. The chef tossed the vegetables into the big pot **simmering** on the stove.

   _____

8. That **simmering** pot looks very **inviting**.

   _____

9. Today's **featured** speaker is from Chile.

   _____

10. She seems to enjoy **making** people angry.

    _____

11. Wandering down the path, he ran across a large toad.

_____

12. After **wandering** down the path, he decided to take a swim.

_____

13. He started **wandering** down the path.

B. **a)** Identify the functions of all PresPartPh-s, PastPartPh-s and GerPh-s.

b) For PresPart-s and PastPart-s, decide if they are heads of PartPh-s or heads of MV;

Answers to Exercises A and B

A   **B**

1. Ger (VT)   head of GerPh "making money": Subj
2. Adj
3. PresPart (VI)   head of PresPartPh "sitting in the back": Adj (modifying "the people")
4. Adj
5. PastPart (VT)   head of the PastPartPh "posted on Wikipedia": Adj
                         (modifying "a great deal of the information")
6. PresPart (VI)   head of MV "was simmering"
7. PresPart (VI)   head of the PresPartPh "simmering on the stove": Adj
                         (modifying "the big pot")
8. Adj; Adj
9. Adj
10. Ger (Vc)   head of the GerPh "making people angry": DO of VT "seems to enjoy"
                         [inside the GerPh: "people" is the DO of Ger, while "angry": OC:Adj]
11. PresPart (VI)   head of the PresPartPh
                         Note: We'll discuss this function of the PresPartPh in Chapter 17.
12. Ger (VI)   head of the GerPh "wandering down the path": Obj/Prep "after"
13. Ger (VI)   head of the GerPh "wandering down the path": DO of VT "started"

Subordinate Clauses and Non-Finite Verbals: Review

Subordinate Clauses and Non-finite Verbal Phrases are structures embedded in main clauses following the principles of subordination, substitution, and modification. Thus, the AdvCl "when they heard voices" is subordinate to (or dependent on) the main clause "they stopped moving" in (1). The NCL "who will finish on time" substitutes (or replaces) an NP like "the result" in (2). The RelCl and the PresPartPh in (3)-(4) modify the NP "the man."

1) $_{AdvCl}$[When they heard voices], they stopped moving.
2) It is hard to tell$_{NCL}$[who will finish on time].
3) The man$_{RelCl}$[who is skating the fastest] is my dad.
4) The man$_{PresPartPh}$[skating the fastest] is my dad.

Subordinate Clauses and Non-finite Verbals help us construct complex sentences and replace or modify NPs.

They have internal structure. Subordinate clauses have clause (i.e., sentence) structure, thus they contain a NP:Subj and VP:Pred. Non-finite verbals are phrases; thus they have the structure of a VP minus tense. The diagrams below show their internal structure. The interrupted line in the diagram for Non-finite verbals indicates that some of them (InfPh-s and GerPh-s) occasionally have explicit subjects.

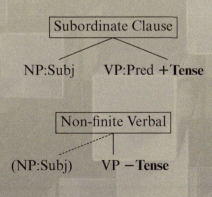

Things You Need to Know About

Subordinate Clauses and Non-finite Verbals

Subordinate clauses function as:

Subordinate Clauses		
Function	Type	Example
Nouns	**NCL (That-Clause)**	**That he finished on time** is surprising. *NCL:Subj*
	NCL (Wh-Clause)	It is hard to tell **who will finish on time.** *NCL:DO of Inf (VT) "tell"*
Adjectives	**RelCl**	I really liked the song **which you wrote last month.** *RelCl:Adj (modifying "the song")*
Adverbs	**AdvCl**	**When they heard voices,** they stopped moving. *AdvCl:Adv-time*

The following is a list of all the NP functions which NPs in general, and NCl-s, InfPh-s, and GerPh-s in particular can have.

NP functions			
All NPs (including NCL-s, InfPh-s, and GerPh-s) in Main and/or Subordinate Clauses		**NCL-s and InfPh-s only**	
	Examples:		Examples:
(1) Subj	**(1)** Skating is fun.	**(7)** Comp to Adj	**(7)** It'll be **great** to go skating.
(2) DO	**(2)** I love skating.		
(3) IO	**(3)** I gave skating my life.	**(8)** Comp to NP (NP:Subj, NP:PredN, etc.)	**(8)** I like **the plan** to go skating on the weekend.
(4) PredN	**(4)** My hobby is skating.		
(5) OC	**(4)** He let me skate all day.		
(6) Obj/Prep	**(6)** I was thinking about skating.		

Things You Need to Know About

Subordinate Clauses and Non-finite Verbals

Non-finite verbals function as:

Non-Finite Verbals		
Type	Function	Example
GerPh	**Nouns**	**Skating fast** is fun. *GerPh:Subj*
InfPh		I am learning **to skate fast.** *NCL:DO of VT "am learning"*
InfPh	**Adverbs**	I am skating **to win this competition.** *InfPh:Adv-reason*
PresPartPh[1]	**? Adverbs**	**Skating flawlessly,** he won his third competition. *PresPartPh:Adv-attendant circumstance*
PastPartPh		**Supported by the cheering crowd,** he skated the skate of his life. *PastPartPh:Adv-reason*
PresPartPh	**Adjectives**	The man **skating the fastest** is my dad. *PresPartPh:Adj (modifying "the man")*
PastPartPh		I remember all the skating competitions **won by Canadian athletes in the last five years.** *PastPartPh:Adj (modifying "all the skating competitions")*

[1]Some grammarians; e.g., Morenberg (2010:194–5) identify this function of PresPartPh-s and PastPartPh-s as Adverbial. We will discuss this issue in more detail in Ch. 17.

Exercises

A. In the following sentences, bracket each Wh-clause. Then underline the WhSub and state its role within the clause (NP:Subj, NP:DO, Adv, etc.). Also state the role of the clause (NP:Subj; NP:DO, etc.) in the sentence.

1. The records will show who was there.

   _____

2. Don explained how the program worked.

   _____

3. Where they live is beautiful.

   _____

4. A good rest is what he needs.

   _____

5. I wonder how often they'll visit us.

   _____

6. I don't know why he did that.

   _____

7. I'll give the sofa to whoever wants it.

   _____

8. He'll cook dinner with whatever we buy.

   _____

9. When we go depends on the weather.

   _____

10. Whatever you cook, I'll eat.

   _____

B. How many Subordinate Clauses and Non-finite Verbals are there in the sentence? Identify each of them by copying it and stating its function.

1. Why don't you let me use the paper you wrote for this course last term?

   _____

   _____

2. I plan to let my assistant go after the holidays.

   _____

   _____

3. A lot of wood was needed to warm up this place.

   _____

   _____

4. The students didn't find working at the zoo a very useful experience.

   _____

   _____

5. After hearing the verdict, the witness realized he had been used to convict an innocent man.

   _____

   _____

6. He came to help organize the event.

   _____

   _____

7. Chris Jordan is a Seattle-based photographer who quantifies consumption via images that reveal exactly how many products are bought or discarded in a given period of time, a minute, an hour, a day, or a year.
   [from the SFU website, events.sfu.ca]

   _____

   _____

8. A new copyright clearance checklist has been created to help clarify how instructors may request copyright compliant reproductions for instructional purposes.
[from "Academic Copyright . . . ," copyright.com]

_____

_____

9. With an elevation of 400 metres above sea level, it's not unusual for the Burnaby campus to be transformed into a winter wonderland.
[from the SFU website, sfu.ca]

_____

_____

10. "Flower Power" helps catch criminals.
[from the SFU website, sfu.ca]

_____

_____

11. The talk will review some of the basic principles of how plants can be used in criminal investigations including murder.
[from the SFU website, sfu.ca]

_____

_____

12. Speakers will talk about poverty, employment, climate change, and building community self-reliance through transforming our food systems to become more socially and environmentally just and sustainable.
[from "Land and Food . . . ," landfood.ubc.ca]

_____

_____

13. The new application called "Eyes and Feet" helps local businesses use social media more effectively by showing how competitors and customers are using it.
[from "Marketing Tips . . . ," reelseo.com]

_____

_____

14. The service integrates Google Maps, Twitter, Facebook, Foursquare, and Groupon to let local businesses get a visual representation of the businesses and customers who are using social media surrounding them.
[from "Marketing Tips . . . ," reelseo.com]

_____

_____

15. SFU was the first Canadian university to establish a forensic laboratory in 1999 that uses entomology—the study of bugs—to help solve murders nationally and internationally.
[from the SFU website, sfu.ca]

_____

_____

Answers to Selected Exercises

B. **1.** Two **(1)** RelCl:Adj "you wrote for this course last term"

(2) InfP:OC of Vc "let"—"use the paper you wrote for this course last term"

2. Two **(1)** InfPh:DO of "plan"—"to let my assistant go after the holidays"

(2) InfPh:OC of "let"—"go"

3. One **(1)** InfPh: Adv-reason (=in order to . . .)—"to warm up (VT) this place"

Note that "was needed" is passive (Aux + VT) from "We needed a lot of wood to warm up this place."

4. One **(1)** GerPh:DO of "didn't find (Vc)"—"working (VI) at the zoo"

5. Three **(1)** GerPh:Obj/Prep "after"—"hearing the verdict"

(2) That-Cl:DO of "realized"—"he had been used to convict an innocent man" (deleted COMP 'that')

(3) InfPh:Adv-reason (=in order to)—"to convict an innocent man"

6. Two **(1)** InfPh:Adv "to help organize the event"

(2) InfPh:DO of "help"—"organize the event"

7. Three **(1)** RelCl:Adj "who quantifies consumption . . . a year"

(2) RelCl:Adj "that reveal exactly how many . . . a year"

(3) Wh-Cl:DO "how many products . . . a year"

8. Three **(1)** InfPh:Adv "to help clarify . . . purposes"

(2) InfPh:DO of "help"—"clarify . . . .purposes"

(3) WhCl:DO of "clarify"—"how instructors . . . purposes"

9. One **(1)** InfPh:Comp to Adj "not unusual"—"for the Burnaby campus to be . . . wonderland"

10. One **(1)** InfPh:DO of "help"—"catch criminals"

11. One   **(1)** NCL:Obj/Prep "of"—"how plants can be used in criminal investigations including murder"

12. Three   **(1)** GerPh:Obj/Prep "about"—"building . . . sustainable"

              (2) GerPh:Obj/Prep "through"—"transforming . . . sustainable"

              (3) InfPh:Adv "to become . . . sustainable"

13. Four   **(1)** PastPartPh:Adj—"called 'Eyes and Feet"

              (2) InfPh:OC of Vc "help"—"use social . . . using it"

              (3) GerPh:Obj/Prep "by"—"showing how . . . using it"

              (4) Wh-Cl:DO of Ger "showing"—"how competitors . . . using it"

14. Four   **(1)** InfPh:Adv-purpose—"to let . . . surrounding them"

              (2) InfPh:OC of Vc "let"—"get a . . . surrounding them"

              (3) RelCl:Adj "who are . . . surrounding them"

              (4) PresPartPh:Adj "surrounding them"

15. Four   **(1)** InfPh:Comp to NP "the first Canadian University"—"to establish . . . internationally"

              (2) RelCl:Adj "that uses entomology . . . internationally"

              (3) InfPh:Adv:"to help . . . internationally"

              (4) InfPh:DO of "help"—"solve . . . internationally"

Restrictive vs. Non-Restrictive Modification

A variety of modifiers, including relative clauses, participial phrases, and prepositional phrases may function as either restrictive or non-restrictive modifiers.

Restrictive modifiers may be seen as restricting or "narrowing down" the range of possible people or things referred to by the noun they modify. Consider the following sentence and its restrictive relative clause:

The bread **that I bought** was stale.

Most people see this sentence as entailing the following notions:

- there are many loaves of bread in the world
- the particular loaf I bought was stale

Here the relative clause restricts the meaning of the subject NP to one particular instance—the one that I bought.

Non-restrictive modifiers do not restrict meaning. Instead, they add additional, non-essential information about the noun they modify. The following sentence contains a non-restrictive relative clause.

Peter Fonda, who starred in *Ulee's Gold,* did not win an Oscar.

Here, the clause does not restrict "Peter Fonda"; it merely supplies incidental information.

Notice that restrictive modifiers are generally not punctuated. Non-restrictive units are set off with commas, dashes, or even parentheses.

NOTE: It is very important to understand that it is not the punctuation of a modifier that "causes" it to be restrictive. Rather, punctuation is used to convey the intended meaning to the reader. Remember that punctuation is merely a convention that is observed in writing and that it is not part of "grammar." In this case, however, there is a close relationship between a punctuation convention and the grammatical structure.

Other examples:

The cat **in the window** has fleas. (restrictive prepositional phrase)
Most cats, **except for Felix**, like catnip. (non-restrictive prepositional phrase)
The cat **sitting in the window** has fleas. (restrictive present participial phrase)
Felix, **sitting in the window and grooming himself**, was a happy cat.
  (non-restrictive present participial phrase)
His wife, **Carol**, is a microbiologist. (non-restrictive appositive; he can't (legally)
  have more than one wife)
His sister **Ellen** is a professor. (restrictive appositive; he has more than one sister,
  and one of them is a professor)
His sister, **Ellen**, is a professor. (non-restrictive appositive; he has one sister, and
  her name is Ellen)

Things You Need to Know About

Restrictive vs. Non-Restrictive Modification

Restrictive modifiers, as the name suggests, limit or restrict the number of referents from a bigger set to a smaller set, often just one referent. Restrictive modifiers include many of the structures discussed in previous chapters such as relative clauses, participial phrases, and prepositional phrases. These restrictive modifiers have **non-restrictive** counterparts which add non-essential information to the sentence, and are added as parenthetical comments or asides.

Restrictive Modifiers	Non-restrictive Modifiers
Restrictive Relative Clauses 1. *Canadians **who believe their economy is doing o.k.** may be surprised by the latest unemployment statistics.* ■ Implies some of them. ■ The meaning is "Some Canadians believe their economy is doing o.k., and they may be surprised by the latest unemployment statistics."	**Non-restrictive Relative Clauses** 2. *Canadians, **who believe their economy is doing o.k.,** may be surprised by the latest unemployment statistics.* ■ Implies all of them. ■ The meaning is "Canadians, all of whom by the way believe their economy is doing o.k., may be surprised by the latest unemployment statistics."
Restrictive Present Participial Phrases 3. *The cat **purring loudly** is my neighbour's.*  ■ Implies there is more than one cat in that setting, and only one is purring loudly; that cat is my neighbour's. ■ Functions as an Adjective. ■ Has a fixed position in the sentence, after the NP it modifies.	**Non-restrictive Present Participial Phrases** **4.a.** ***Purring loudly,** the cat jumped into my lap.* **4.b.** *The cat jumped into my lap, **purring loudly**.* ■ Implies there is one cat, who was purring loudly while it jumped into my lap. ■ Introduces a simultaneous activity, and some grammarians call it an Adverb of attendant circumstance (Morenberg 2010:194); however, this view is controversial. In the model sentence, for example, the PresPartPh is still saying something about the cat; i.e., modifying it. ■ As 4.b. shows, it can be moved around freely in the sentence.

Images courtesy of shutterstock.com

Things You Need to Know About

Restrictive vs. Non-Restrictive Modification

Restrictive Modifiers	Non-restrictive Modifiers

Restrictive Past Participial Phrases

5. *Motorcycles* **made in Japan** *are usually reliable and durable.*

- Helps identify the referents.

- (5) states that only those motorcycles which are made in Japan are reliable and durable; it does not make the same claim about motorcycles made elsewhere.

7. *Students* **overwhelmed by the amount of required reading** *usually drop the course.*

- Restricts the referents from all students to just those who get overwhelmed by the amount of reading.

- Functions as an Adjective.

- Is bound to its NP.

Non-restrictive Past Participial Phrases

6. *The motorcycles,* **made in Japan,** *survived two of the Paris-Dakar rallies.*

- Provides additional information, which is not essential for identifying the referents.

- The use of the DefArt with "motorcycles" suggests the listener/reader can identify them; the PastPartPh means "By the way, these motorcycles were made in Japan."

8. ***Overwhelmed by the amount of required reading,** the students decided to drop the course.*

$$A \Rightarrow B$$

- Introduces a causal relation similar to an AdvCl with "because"—"The students decided to drop the course because they were overwhelmed by the amount of reading."

- Some grammarians call it an Adverb of reason (Morenberg 2010:194–5); however, as the model sentences show, the PastPartPh is still saying something about the motorcycles in (6) and the students in (8).

- Can move around in the sentence.

Images courtesy of shutterstock.com

Things You Need to Know About	
Restrictive vs. Non-Restrictive Modification	

Restrictive Modifiers	Non-restrictive Modifiers
Restrictive Prepositional Phrases 9. *The people **at the end of the line** were getting impatient.* ■ Suggests that the people who were at the end of the line were getting impatient, but does not make such a claim about others. ■ Can be viewed as a reduced RelCl with a deleted RelPro and MV "BE." ■ The PP is bound to the NP "the people." ■ Functions as an Adjective.	**Non-restrictive Prepositional Phrases** 10. ***With or without the teachers' support,** the parents were determined to fight the School Board's decision to cancel Art classes.* ■ Introduces an additional comment on the sentence as a whole. ■ The PP is not bound to any particular phrase in the sentence (can move freely). ■ Functions as an Adverb of accompaniment.
Restrictive Appositives 11. *His sister **Ellen** is a professor.* ■ The Appositive NP "Ellen" singles out one of his sisters as the referent. ■ (11) implies he has more than one sister, and one of them, called Ellen, is a professor.	**Non-restrictive Appositives (NPs or AdjPs)** 12. *His sister, **Ellen,** is a professor.* ■ The Appositive NP "Ellen" repeats or states differently the information in the NP "his sister." ■ (12) implies that he has one sister, whose name is Ellen, and she is a professor.
Images courtesy of shutterstock.com	

Things You Need to Know About
Restrictive vs. Non-Restrictive Modification

Restrictive Modifiers	Non-restrictive Modifiers
	13. *Talented and ambitious, his sister got an Ivy League degree.* ■ The Appositive AdjP provides non-restrictive modification for the NP "his sister." ■ Can move around in the sentence. ■ When the Appositive AdjP is placed before rather than after the NP it modifies, as in (13), it seems to introduce a causal relationship (similar to that in (8)), "Because she was talented and ambitious, his sister got an Ivy League degree." **Absolute Phrases** ■ Absolute Phrases contain NP:Subjects and partial predicates without tense. ■ The partial predicates are frequently participial phrases. ■ Absolute phrases can be derived by deleting the MV BE or AUX BE from a clause, thus deleting tense. 14. *The crowd continued to push its way forward to the stage, the police unable to stop it.* ■ In (14), "the police" is the NP:Subject (underlined), and "unable to stop it" is the partial predicate. ■ The Absolute can be derived by deleting the MV BE and with it, its tense; e.g., "the police ~~was~~ unable to stop it." <div align="center">**Absolute** NP:Subj Partial Predicate (-tense) **the police** ~~**was**~~ **unable to stop it**</div>

Restrictive Modifiers	Non-restrictive Modifiers

	Absolutes with "With"
	
	■ Absolutes often occur with the word "with", which functions like a Subord rather than a Prep, as in (15):
	
	15. *With **gas prices going up**, people will be moving to more fuel-efficient cars.*
	
	   ■ Absolutes with "with" need to be distinguished from Non-restrictive PP with the Prep "with"; compare (15) and (16):
	
	16. *With **higher gas prices**, people will be moving to more fuel-efficient cars.*
	
	   ■ The Absolute with "with" in (15) has an NP: Subject ("gas prices") and a predicate without tense ("going up"), while the PP with "with" in (16) has only an NP ("higher gas prices").
	
	   ■ Like all other restrictive and non-restrictive modifiers, absolute phrases can be compound, and can contain embedded elements; consider (18) derived from (17):
	
	With
	↓
	
	17. *Salaries ~~have been~~ going down, and inflation ~~has been~~ going up in the last six month. So, many university graduates have been willing to accept low-paid jobs.*
	
	With
	↓
	
	18. ***salaries going down, and inflation going up in the last six months***_[Cpd Absolutes], *many university graduates have been willing to accept low-paid jobs.*
	
	   ■ Finally, compare (18) to (19), which contains another NonRest PP with the Prep "with":
	
	19. ***With lower salaries and higher inflation***_[Cpd NonRestPPs], *many university graduates have been willing to accept low-paid jobs.*

Exercises

A. Determine whether the modifying phrases and clauses are restrictive or non-restrictive and punctuate appropriately.

1. The tallest building in Toronto the CN Tower is an important landmark.

_____

2. Robertson Davies' novel Fifth Business is the first book of the Deptford Trilogy.

_____

3. Vancouver which is the third largest city in Canada is on the west coast.

_____

4. The Vancouver in Washington is much smaller.

_____

5. Sir John A. Macdonald who is depicted on the ten-dollar bill was known for his heavy drinking.

_____

6. The university claiming the largest number of library holdings per student is the University of Alberta.

_____

7. The man who is depicted on the five-dollar bill is Laurier.

_____

8. Beethoven's opera Fidelio is a masterpiece.

_____

9. People who live in glass houses shouldn't throw stones.

_____

10. Because the guests never arrived, all the work I did on Thursday the cooking, the cleaning, and the fluffing of the pillows was a waste of time.

_____

B. Choose one of the following labels that best describes the underlined word or group of words. If a group of words is not a sentence modifier; e.g., if it a RestRelCl rather than a NonRestRelCl, write None.

Absolute	NonRestPastPartPh
AdvCl	NonRestPP
Appositive AdjP	NonRestPresPartPh
Appositive NP	NonRestRelCl
None	

1. When he woke up, it was still raining, **the raindrops quietly tapping on the kitchen window**.

_____

2. People often throw the wrong things into the wrong containers—**making recyclables useless and a big mess for us to clean up**.

_____

3. The United States and China, **by far the world's two biggest polluters**, have the technology and processes in place right now to accurately measure and report their emissions of CO_2 and other heat-trapping gases.
[adapted from "Sustainable World . . . ," sustainableworld.org.uk]

_____

4. SFU Surrey mechatronics student Ben Brown-Bentley, **who runs the event company Adrenaline Productions**, is the city of Surrey's latest student entrepreneur of the year.
[from the SFU website, sfu.ca]

_____

5. **Commonly considered a grain**, quinoa is a seed which is related to leafy green vegetables such as spinach, chard, and beets.

_____

6. "From C to C: Chinese Canadian Stories of Migration"—**a richly layered exploration of the fate of pioneer Chinese-Canadians through the eyes of their descendants**—will eventually be televised to viewers worldwide.

_____

7. Kids **that are involved in helping plan and prepare a meal** are more likely to sit down and enjoy it.

   _____

8. **With weather-watchers betting on the coldest and snowiest B.C. winter in decades**, it's time to think about winter travel on Burnaby Mountain.
   [from the SFU website, sfu.ca]

   _____

9. **Before you drive on Burnaby Mountain**, check the SFU Road Conditions report online or by phone at 604-444-4929.
   [from the SFU website, sfu.ca]

   _____

10. Let's remember some of these students are quite young and brash, and **being far from home**, have little if any supervision.

    _____

11. **For some reason**, students have been finding it absolutely impossible to walk over to the garbage can to throw things out.

    _____

12. Eventually, A.J.'s conduct, **shameful and disgraceful not just for his employer but for the entire industry**, led to the club's bankruptcy.

    _____

13. **Amused by the cat's relentless effort to catch his tail while spinning**, Jeremy came up with an idea for his next animation movie.

    _____

14. I dislike the dumbing down of many toys **marketed to females** and the fact that a lot of toys for girls involve passive role-playing rather than a decision-making adventure focus.
    [from Together Family, togetherfamily.ca]

    _____

15. **With little ones running around**, we know you are constantly doing laundry.
[from Together Family, togetherfamily.ca]

_____

16. Students **who do not pass this exam** may fail the course.

_____

Answers to Selected Exercises

B. **1.** Absolute
2. NonRestPresPartPh
3. Appositive NP
4. NonRestRelCl
5. NonRestPastPartPh
6. Appositive NP
7. None   [RestRelCl]
8. Absolute
9. AdvCl
10. NonRestPresPartPh
11. NonRest PP
12. Appositive AdjP
13. NonRestPastPartPh
14. None   [RestPastPartPh]
15. Absolute
16. None   [RestRelCl]

Identifying Errors Made by Second Language Learners

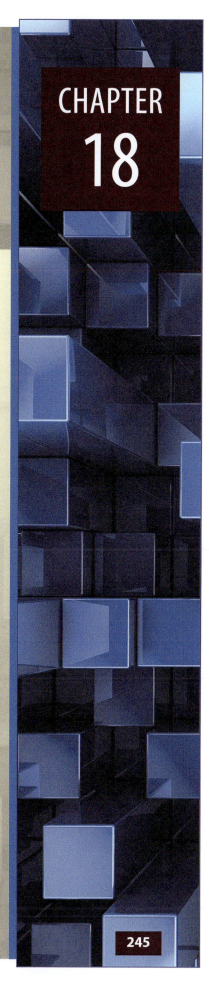

The study of errors made by second language (L2) learners is a complex field of research that is of great interest to applied linguists. When we use the term "errors" we generally mean patterns of language that learners use, but that have not typically occurred in the input they have received, and that would not be used by proficient speakers of the language. For instance, someone who says *"*He goed"* may do so without ever having heard anyone use that pattern before. Instead, the verb form is likely to have been constructed by the learner on the basis of incomplete knowledge of English. Many errors in L2 speech and writing appear to arise in this way. Other errors may occur because L2 learners inappropriately apply patterns from their native language in their L2. A speaker of French, for example, might say, *"*I carry often my umbrella with me."* Speakers of WCE consider this sentence ungrammatical because adverbs do not normally occur between a VT and a following NP:DO in English. And once again, this pattern is unlikely to occur in the input received by English learners. However, French *does* allow the pattern VT + Adv + NP:DO. In this case, then, the learner's knowledge of French appears to have *interfered* with L2 learning.

It is interesting to note that many L2 learners never reach a point of fully "native-like" language use. In other words, the outcome of L2 acquisition is often different from that of L1 acquisition. But even when L2 learners do not produce language that is identical to native speakers' language, they may still be excellent communicators. For that reason, it is very important not to regard the language of L2 users as "defective" or "inferior" simply because it is different from L1 language.

All the examples below illustrate matters that might be covered in courses for learners of English as a second language. They are presented here to give you an idea of the range of difficulties that English L2 speakers experience, and to provide you with analytical tools that you can use if you ever find yourself teaching English.

1. Choice of Verb Tense, Aspect, or Voice.

Joe *has called* me at 6:00 yesterday.

> *Target form:* Joe *called* me
> *Explanation:* The present perfect is not generally used when an exact time is specified in the sentence.

Linda *has been* married for several years, but she died last month.

> *Target form:* was married, had been married
> *Explanation:* The present perfect usually indicates an action or state that continues to be true up to the moment of speaking. If we say "Linda has been married for several years," we are implying that she is still married. Therefore, the present perfect is not appropriate in the first part of the sentence.

This broken chair needs to *fix*.

> *Target form:* needs to *be fixed*
> *Explanation:* In the intended utterance, the chair is not an agent. Rather the agent is unspecified ("Unspecified" is the one who will fix the chair). To convey this meaning, a passive construction is needed ("The chair needs to be fixed by unspecified").

2. Verb Forms

Note: These errors differ from tense, aspect, or voice errors in that they result in an impossible verb form.

Did *he* left *yet*?

> *Target form:* *Did* he *leave* yet?
> *Explanation:* "Did left" is not a grammatical structure. Here the past tense has been marked twice. It can be marked only once.

When I called, she *was work* on her project.

> *Target form:* *was working*
> *Explanation:* "Was work" is not grammatical. The past progressive must be marked with—ing.

He *drived* to the movie.

> *Target form:* *drove*
> *Explanation:* Proficient speakers generally don't consider "drived" to be the past form of "drive."

3. Problems with the Number of a Noun (Singular vs. Plural)

Helen was able to obtain *many interesting informations* from her new CD-ROM.

Target form: a great deal of interesting *information*
Explanation: In this context "information" is an uncountable noun. It cannot be pluralized or determined by the PreArt "many."

She bought some new *softwares* for her computer.

Target form: software
Explanation: In this context "software" is an uncountable noun. It cannot be pluralized.

4. Subject-Verb Agreement
The guys was busy in the work room.

Target form: *were* busy
Explanation: The subject of the sentence ("the guys . . .") is plural. The verb must therefore be plural.

5. Gerund-Infinitive Confusion
Tom enjoys *to cook* when he has the time.

Target form: cooking
Explanation: "Enjoys" requires a gerund object. It cannot take an infinitive.

6. Word Order Errors
Why *you don't* come to visit me more often?

Target form: don't you
Explanation: In question formation, "do" and other auxiliaries must be moved to the front of the clause, in this case after the Wh-word (inversion).

Frank *called up her* to invite her to the party.

Target form: called her up
Explanation: When separable two-word verbs (such as "call up") have a personal pronoun object, that object must appear between the verb and particle.

Carol picked up *large two watermelons* at the market.

Target form: two large watermelons
Explanation: Normally CardN (e.g., "two") must precede any adjectives modifying a noun.

Ted *gets usually up* early.

Target form: usually gets up early
Explanation: It is generally not possible to break up a two-word verb with an adverbial expression.

I bought *yesterday* a litre of milk.

> ***Target form:*** *Yesterday,* I bought a litre of milk. I bought a litre of milk *yesterday.*
> ***Explanation:*** Adverbial expressions cannot occur between a VT and its DO.

7. Difficult Prepositions
Note: The correct preposition for a particular context often cannot be predicted from any "rule." Instead prepositions tend to be used idiomatically.

I was born *in* September 24, 1982.

> ***Target form:*** on (used for exact dates)

I was born *on* September.

> ***Target form:*** in (used for months)

He is studying *in* SFU.

> ***Target form:*** at (used for a particular school or other institution)

8. Problems with Do-Support
Why you said that?

> ***Target form:*** *Why did you say* that?
> ***Explanation:*** Questions in which there is no auxiliary or BE require do-support.

Tomorrow's a holiday, so I *haven't to* go to work.

> ***Target form:*** I *don't have to*
> ***Explanation:*** The catenative "have to" cannot be negated as a contraction. It requires "do-support." (don't have to)

9. Miscellaneous Problems
Phone *to* me tomorrow if you have time.

> ***Target form:*** *Phone me*
> ***Explanation:*** "Phone" in the sense of "phone someone" is a VT and requires a DO, not a prepositional phrase.

The runner *won the race* was from China.

> ***Target form:*** The runner *who won the race*
> ***Explanation:*** It is not possible to delete a RelPro (who) in a relative clause when it plays the role of Subj within the RELCL.

The hotel which I stayed in *it* last year was very good.

> **Target form:** The hotel *that I stayed in* last year.
> **Explanation:** "Which" is a RelPro playing the role of Obj/Prep (of the preposition "in"). It is redundant (and ungrammatical) to use "it" as an Obj/Prep in the same clause. "It" and "which" would be playing the same role.

The clerk *which* sold me the shirt is not working today.

> **Target form:** *who*
> **Explanation:** "Which" cannot be used for a human referent.

Things You Need to Know About

Common Errors Made by ESL Learners

The following table includes some common types of errors made by ESL learners, categorized according to the main grammar structures introduced in this text. Some space is left for you to include other common errors you have noticed.

General Category	Subcategories	Specific Errors and Examples
(1) Verb Phrase	**(1)** Verb type and verb complements	**(1)** Using "BE" + PredAdj instead of a VT, such as agree as in *He is agreed.*
	(2) Verb tense and aspect	**(2)** present perfect used with a specific date in time as in *He **has been** there in 1996.*
	(3) Other. Specify.	
(2) Noun Phrase	**(1)** Order of elements within the NP	**(1)** placing OrdN before CardN as in *the **two first** guys in line*
	(2) Count vs. Non-count nouns	**(2)** using a non-count noun as a count in *I have job experience**s** working as a teacher.* But note the correct *Ever since I came to Canada, I have had many positive experiences.*
	(3) Subject-Verb Agreement (SVA)	**(3)** Lack of SVA *My landlady **know** how to cook.*
	(4) Other. Specify.	

	Things You Need to Know About Common Errors Made by ESL Learners	
General Category	**Subcategories**	**Specific Errors and Examples**
(3) Rearranging and Compounding	**(1)** Word Order (WO) in questions	**(1)** Adv of frequency "ever" placed before the DO rather than the PastPart of the V "seen" in *Have you seen **ever** such a thing?*
	(2) WO in indirect questions	**(2)** InterProAdv V Subj rather than InterProAdv Subj V in indirect questions like *Do you know where **is he**?*
	(3) Mistakes with passive forms	**(3)** Missing Aux Be: e.g., *The building ____ demolished two months ago by the contractors.*
	(4) Other. Specify.	
(4) Subordinate Clauses	**(1)** Relative Clauses	**(1)** repeating the IO in the RelCl with a Pro (where a blank should be left) as in *I know the man who she gave it to **him**.*
	(2) Adverbial Clauses	**(2)** use of Prep "despite" instead of SubordConj "although" in ***Despite** he had difficulties, he managed to graduate in May.*
	(3) Noun Clauses **(a)** That-clauses	**(3)** Verb specific complementation **(a)** Using a That-Cl instead of InfPh as in *He wants **that he goes on a vacation**.*
	(b) Wh-clauses	**(b)** Filling the Adv slot in the Wh-Cl twice as in *I don't know where he went **there**.*
	(4) Other. Specify.	

	Things You Need to Know About	
	Common Errors Made by ESL Learners	
General Category	**Subcategories**	**Specific Errors and Examples**
(5) Prepositional and Participial Phrases	**(1)** PP	**(1)** The verb "be" must be deleted in a PP *The cup **was** in front of him had lipstick on it.*
	(2) PresPartPh	**(2)** Verb "contains" needs to be made into PresPart (or a RelCl must be used) as in *The letter **contains** the threat is from them.*
	(3) PastPartPh	**(3)** The verb "be" needs to be deleted in a PastPartPh *The lady **was** dressed in black looked at him.*
	(4) Other. Specify.	
(6) Gerunds and Infinitives	**(1)** Gerunds	**(1)** Using infinitives instead of gerunds *He avoids to drive at night.*
	(2) Infinitives	**(2)** Using gerunds instead of infinitives *He helped me finding the way.*
	(3) Other. Specify.	
(7) Other. Specify.		

Remember that English sentences are made up of slots. You can think of them as templates, or empty boxes which have relatively fixed places in the sentence and with respect to each other. These slots or boxes can be filled with as few as one word each, or with much longer sequences of words.

Look at the following examples from the cover of this text. The Blue boxes contain the NP:Subjects, the red ones contain the Main Verbs, and the blue boxes framed in red contain NPs (hence the blue colour) which are complements of the verb (hence the red colour).

If you understand this concept, you will be able to manipulate a larger number of structures to express a given meaning.

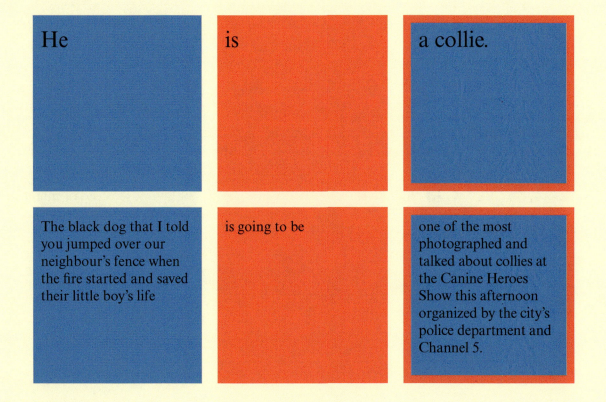

He	is	a collie.
The black dog that I told you jumped over our neighbour's fence when the fire started and saved their little boy's life	is going to be	one of the most photographed and talked about collies at the Canine Heroes Show this afternoon organized by the city's police department and Channel 5.

If you can analyze the elements of the second sentence, you have done a great job learning the fundamentals of English grammar. Congratulations! You are now a better writer, a better speaker, a better editor, a better ESL student or teacher, a better everything!

Supplementary Material: Tense, Aspect, and Modal Sequences

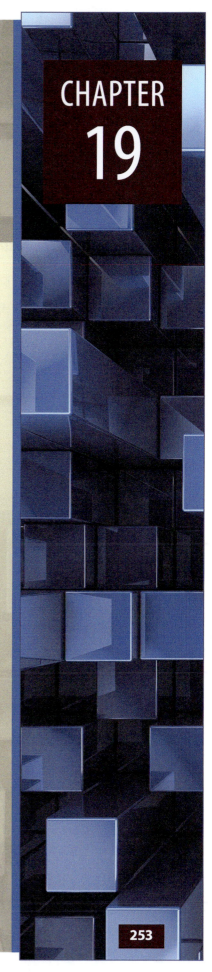

CHAPTER

19

The following examples illustrate some of the common tense, aspect, and modal sequences. These patterns should not be viewed as "rules" or advice on the "correct" forms. In fact, many other patterns are possible.

I. Conditional Sentences

Possible present or future condition

> if clause: simple present, present continuous
> result clause: will (future time), present continuous (future time),
>   imperative, simple present (habitual)

>> If it's raining right now, we'll get our umbrellas.
>> If it rains tomorrow, we'll take our umbrellas.
>> If it rains tomorrow, I'm taking my umbrella.
>> If it rains, take your umbrella.
>> If it rains, I take my umbrella.

Present contrary-to-fact condition

> if clause: simple past, past continuous
> result clause: would, could

>> If it were raining, we would get our umbrellas.
>> If we were in Paris, we could visit the Louvre.

Past true condition

> if clause: simple past, past continuous
> result clause: past tense

>> If it was sunny, we always ate outside.

Past contrary-to-fact condition

if clause: past perfect, past perfect continuous
result clause: would have, could have

If it had rained, we would have gotten our umbrellas.
If we had taken more money, we could have stayed longer.

II. Direct Quotations and Reported Speech

In reported speech, the simple present and present progressive may be replaced by simple past and past progressive.

Marilyn said, "The flowers are beautiful."
Marilyn said that the flowers were beautiful.

Joan commented, "It's raining."
Joan commented that it was raining.

The simple past, past progressive, and present perfect may be replaced by the past perfect. The past perfect remains unchanged.

He said, "I slept well last night."
He said that he had slept well last night.

She replied, "I was working at the office on Sunday"
She replied that she had been working at the office on Sunday.

Don shouted, "The pipe has burst."
Don shouted that the pipe had burst.

Dave said, "The pipe had burst (when I arrived)."
Dave said that the pipe had burst (when he arrived).

"Will" may be replaced by "would," "can" may be replaced by "could."

Diane said, "I'll call you tomorrow."
Diane said that she would call me tomorrow.

Mike boasted, "I can speak five languages."
Mike boasted that he could speak five languages.

III. Other Cases

Interesting patterns occur in *that* clauses preceded by *wish*.

You are here.
I wish (that) you were here.

You will leave.
I wish (that) you would leave.

List of Labels and Parsing Conventions

List I: Alphabetical List of Labels to be Used in Parsing Exercises

Label	Part of speech	Example
Adj	adjective	a **happy** goat
Adv	adverb	Miss Muffett left **suddenly**.
Aux	auxiliary (type unspecified)	Miss Muffett **has** left.
BE	be functioning as a main verb	Little Boy Blue **is** lazy.
CardN	cardinal number	**three** crows
Caten	catenative auxiliary	We **have to** leave.
COMP	complementizer	I think **that** Mr. McGregor is angry.
CoordConj	coordinating conjunction	Jack **and** Jill
Correl	correlative conjunction	**Both** Jack **and** Jill
DefArt	definite article	**the** answer
DemonD	demonstrative determiner	**This** grammar book is interesting.
DemonPro	demonstrative pronoun	**This** is a beautiful castle.
DiscPrt	discourse particle	**Well**? . . . what do you think of my new coat?
Expl	expletive	**It** is obvious that Cinderella is unhappy.
GenN	genitive noun	**Carol's** spinning wheel
Ger	gerund	**Skiing** is popular in BC.
IndefArt	indefinite article	**an** answer
IndPossPro	independent possessive pronoun	**Mine** is over there.
Inf	infinitive	**To live** is to suffer.
Interj	interjection	**Ouch**! I cut my finger.
IntPro	interrogative pronoun	**What** is under the chesterfield?
IntProAdv	interrogative pro-adverb	**Where** do you live?
IntProD	interrogative pro-determiner	**Which** pig tricked the wolf?
Modal	modal auxiliary	Parrots **can** sometimes speak.
N	noun (type unspecified)	**book**, **chair**, **sky**, **anger**
NEG	negative marker	She's **not** here. She isn**'t** here.

Label	Part of speech	Example
OrdN	ordinal number	the **third** little pig
PastPart	past participle	The house **damaged** by the wolf was made of straw.
PossProD	possessive pronoun determiner	**my** work
PostN	postnominal modifier	The kids **both** went up the hill.
PreArt	prearticle	Bo-Peep has **a lot of** sheep.
Prep	preposition	**to** the moon
PresPart	present participle	The cat **sitting** in the window is Bill.
Pro	pronoun (type unspecified)	**he**, **him**, **someone**, **anybody**, **themselves**
PropN	proper noun	**Calgary**, **Alice Munro**
Prt	particle	He got **up** at six.
Qual	qualifier	It's **very** dark.
RelDet	relative determiner	The girl **whose** grandmother was eaten was Red Riding Hood.
RelProAdv	relative pro-adverb	The place **where** she lived was the forest.
RelPro	relative pronoun	The person **who** gave her the cloak was her mother.
RS	reaction signal	Are you finished? . . . **Yes**.
SubConj	subordinating conjunction	**After** he had his accident, Humpty couldn't pull himself together.
Vc	two-place verb having an objective complement	Little pigs **consider** wolves dangerous.
Vg	two-place verb having an indirect object	The man **gave** the little pig a bunch of straw.
VI	intransitive verb	The troll **waited** under the bridge.
VL	linking verb	The troll **seemed** ugly.
VT	transitive verb	Mary **ate** a little lamb with mint sauce.
WhSub	wh-subordinator	**What** the troll wanted was some goat meat.

List II: Noun Phrases

Possible Roles for Noun Phrases	
NP:Subj	**The wolf** chased the pigs.
NP:DO	Goldilocks tasted **the porridge**.
NP:IO	Mary fed **the lambs** some grain. Mary fed some grain to **the lambs**.
NP:PredN	Tom was **a thief**.
NP:OC	The wolf considered grandmother **an old fool**.
NP:Adv	**Last night** the geese started an uprising.
NP:Obj/Prep	The fox climbed over **the fence**.

Special Types of Noun Phrases	
Gerund NP	Wolves like **eating fresh food**.
Infinitive NP	Sheep hate **to be original**.
that-clause NP	Mary believed **that her lamb was intelligent**.
wh-clause NP	The sheep did **what they were told**.

List III: Prepositional Phrases

Types of Prepositional Phrases	
PP:Adj	The cow **in the field** is ours.
PP:Adv(type)	The cow is grazing **in the field**.
PP:Gen	The Prime Minister visited the Queen **of England**.

List IV: Labels for Other Phrase Types

AdjP	adjective phrase	She is **unbelievably beautiful**.
AdvP	adverbial phrase	I saw it **right here**.
VP	verb phrase	I **saw it right here.**
AbsolPh	absolute phrase	**With the bank sector struggling to recover from the latest financial fiasco,** they can't approve any more unreasonable loans.
ApposPh	appositive phrase	My father, **James Keenan,** wrote a letter of recommendation for her.
GerPh	gerund phrase	Wolves like **eating fresh food.**
InfPh	infinitive phrase	Sheep hate **to be original.**
PartPh	participial phrase	The girl **waving at me** is my sister. and **Waving at me,** she walked away.

List V: Clause Types

(no label)	independent clause	When I got my paycheck, **I bought this new pair of shoes.**
ADVCL	(dependent) adverb clause	**When I got my paycheck,** I bought this new pair of shoes.
NCL	(dependent) noun clause	Mary believed **that her lamb was intelligent.**
RELCL	(dependent) relative clause	The person **who gave her the cloak** was her mother.

List VI: Some Parsing Conventions

- Use a single label + "x wds" for multi-word expressions such as catenatives:

  Caten(2 wds)
  I **have to** go now.

- Names of specific people, places, events, etc. that consist of more than one word should be parsed as PropN(x wds):

  PropN(2 wds)
  He has met **Queen Elizabeth**.
                    PropN(2 wds)
  He went to the beach on **Labour Day**.

- Contractions can be denoted by a ' + ' sign.

  Pro + BE
  He's really busy.
   Modal + NEG
  I **wouldn't** want to bother him.

- Use a single label for hyphenated words:

              Adj
  Is this approach **cost-effective**?

- If a proper noun is also genitive, use GenN:

  GenN
  Jake's brother is coming over.

- Write your answers in the activities legibly. Note especially the difference between VI, VT, and VL.

Crystal, David. *The Cambridge Encyclopaedia of the English Language.* Cambridge, New York, Melbourne: Cambridge University Press, 1995. Print.

Language Log. Web. 2 June 2011. <http://languagelog.ldc.upenn.edu/nll>.

Merriam-Webster Online Dictionary. Web. 2 June 2011. <http://www.merriam-webster.com/help/faq/history.htm>.

Morenberg, Max. *Doing Grammar.* 4th ed. New York: Oxford University Press, 2010. Print.

Rodby, Judith, and W. Ross Winterowd. *The Uses of Grammar.* Oxford: Oxford University Press, 2005. Print.

Stewart, Jr., Thomas W., and Nathan Vaillette, eds. *Language Files: Materials for an Introduction to Language and Linguistics.* 8th ed. Columbus, Ohio: The Ohio State University Press, 2001.

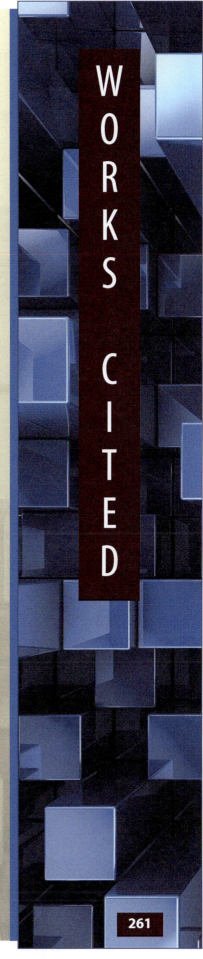

WORKS CITED

This book is designed to help you understand the composition of English sentences and how English language works. It will introduce you to the terminology and concepts commonly used in traditional English grammatical analysis: parts of speech, several main categories of verb types and their complements in English, the elements of a noun phrase, and the parts of simple sentences in English. It will demystify terms like constituency, dependent clauses, independent clauses, and sentence-level embedding, and enable you to use these as building blocks to make compound and complex sentences.

The text has an informal theoretical orientation, and adopts a descriptive rather than prescriptive approach. Using colours, tables, pictures, useful summaries of main points in the "Things You Need to Know" sections, and fascinating diagrams, it will walk you through the process of taking sentences apart, labeling and identifying the various elements of English sentences. It will give you an advanced understanding of style, and the mechanisms available to you to become a better writer, speaker, (self-) editor, or ESL teacher.

The concepts covered in this book are of particular use to teachers of English as a second language, to those planning to take university-level linguistics courses, and to everyone who needs to achieve a higher level of clarity and accuracy in English.